CREATING
the covenant

Participant Guide

Episodes 1–8

Abingdon Press

COVENANT BIBLE STUDY
CREATING THE COVENANT: PARTICIPANT GUIDE

Copyright © 2014 by Abingdon Press

This book is printed on acid-free paper.

ISBN 978-1-4267-7216-0

Scripture quotations are from the Common English Bible. Copyright © 2011 by the Common English Bible. All rights reserved. Used by permission. www.CommonEnglishBible.com.

Printed in the United States of America

14 15 16 17 18 19 20 21 22 23—10 9 8 7 6 5 4 3 2

Covenant Bible Study resources include:

Creating the Covenant: Participant Guide, ISBN 978-1-4267-7216-0 (large print ISBN 978-1-63088-625-7)
Living the Covenant: Participant Guide, ISBN 978-1-4267-7217-7 (large print ISBN 978-1-63088-626-4)
Trusting the Covenant: Participant Guide, ISBN 978-1-4267-7218-4 (large print ISBN 978-1-63088-627-1)
Covenant Bible Study App: Participant Guides for iOS and Android, ISBN 978-1-4267-7219-1

Covenant Bible Study: Covenant Meditations, ISBN 978-1-4267-7220-7
Covenant Bible Study: Covenant Meditations ePub, ISBN 978-1-4267-7221-4
Covenant Bible Study App: Covenant Meditations for iOS and Android, ISBN 978-1-4267-7222-1

Covenant Bible Study: Leader Guide, ISBN 978-1-4267-7223-8
Covenant Bible Study: Leader Guide ePub, ISBN 978-1-4267-7225-2
Covenant Bible Study App: Leader Guide for iOS and Android, ISBN 978-1-4267-7224-5

Covenant Bible Study: DVD Video (set of three), ISBN 978-1-4267-8678-5
Covenant Bible Study: MP4 Video Episodes (download individually from CovenantBibleStudy.com)

CEB Study Bible, hardcover ISBN 978-1-6092-6028-6, decotone ISBN 978-1-6092-6040-8
CEB Study Bible: Large Print Edition, hardcover ISBN 978-1-60926-176-4

To order resources or to obtain additional information for participants, Covenant groups, and leaders, go to www.CovenantBibleStudy.com or to www.cokesbury.com. All print resources are available exclusively from these online sites, from Cokesbury reps, or by calling Cokesbury (800-672-1789). The Covenant Bible Study digital app is available from iTunes and Google Play.

Contents

Other Covenant Participant Guides

CREATING
the covenant

Covenant Group Participants and Leader

Name	Phone	E-mail

Covenant Group Meeting Location _____

Covenant Group Meeting Day and Time _____

CovenantBibleStudy.com username _____ password _____

Bible Readings at a Glance

Sign up with your group at CovenantBibleStudy.com to get daily readings by e-mail from your group leader.

Episode 2

Day 1	Genesis 1–3	Creation and the human role within it	❏
Day 2	Genesis 6:5–9:17; 11:1-9	End of the old world—beginning of the new world	❏
Day 3	Genesis 12; 15; 17; 22	Abraham and nationhood	❏
Day 4	Genesis 27–28; 32–33	Jacob and the biblical family	❏
Day 5	Genesis 37; 41; 43; 45; 50	Joseph and his brothers in Egypt	❏
Day 6	Covenant Meditation on Genesis 1:26-31	Who are we?	❏
Day 7	Group Meeting Experience with Genesis 9:7-17	The Bible's first covenant	❏

Episode 3

Day 1	Exodus 1–4	Oppression, survival, and the charge of a leader	❏
Day 2	Exodus 13:17–15:21	Crossing boundaries for freedom	❏
Day 3	Exodus 20–24	Sinai covenant	❏
Day 4	Leviticus 19–22	Holiness Code	❏
Day 5	Numbers 11–14	In the wilderness	❏
Day 6	Covenant Meditation on Leviticus 19:1-2	You must be holy because God is holy.	❏
Day 7	Group Meeting Experience with Exodus 20:1-17	Ten Commandments	❏

Episode 4

❑	Day 1	Mark 1–4	God's kingdom is near.
❑	Day 2	Mark 12–14	God's kingdom is not here yet.
❑	Day 3	Matthew 4–7	New instruction for a new kingdom
❑	Day 4	Matthew 11–13	New way of life
❑	Day 5	Matthew 18–22	Jesus is the new Teacher.
❑	Day 6	Covenant Meditation on Mark 10:13-16	God's kingdom belongs to people like these.
❑	Day 7	Group Meeting Experience with Matthew 9:18-33	Jesus as deliverer

Episode 5

❑	Day 1	Romans 1–3	God's solution for the human condition
❑	Day 2	Galatians 1:1–3:5; 5:2-12	The sufficiency of Christ's sacrifice for salvation
❑	Day 3	Galatians 3:6–4:7; Romans 4	Righteousness: Abraham's trust in God's promise
❑	Day 4	Romans 5–8; Galatians 5:13-25	Reconciliation with God; freedom in the Spirit
❑	Day 5	Romans 9–11	God's faithfulness to Israel
❑	Day 6	Covenant Meditation on Galatians 3:23-29	All are one in Christ Jesus.
❑	Day 7	Group Meeting Experience with Romans 14:1–15:2	Practicing grace

Episode 6

❑	Day 1	Hebrews 1–2; Psalm 8	Praise for God's Son
❑	Day 2	Hebrews 3–4; Numbers 14	Faithfulness and loyalty
❑	Day 3	Hebrews 4:14–7:28; Psalm 110	Jesus is our covenant mediator.
❑	Day 4	Hebrews 8:1–10:18; Leviticus 16	Jesus grants us entrance to the most holy place.
❑	Day 5	Hebrews 10:19–13:25	Faith hall of fame
❑	Day 6	Covenant Meditation on Hebrews 6:10-11	Grateful love serves.
❑	Day 7	Group Meeting Experience with Hebrews 5:11–6:12	Honor

Episode 7

Day 1	1 Corinthians 1–4	Immature boasting	❏
Day 2	1 Corinthians 7–10	My freedom is good, but it's not always good for others.	❏
Day 3	1 Corinthians 11–14	No person is better than another.	❏
Day 4	1 Corinthians 15; 2 Corinthians 1:1-11; 4–6	Our faith is pointless without Christ's resurrection.	❏
Day 5	1 Corinthians 16; 2 Corinthians 7–9	Cheerful generosity	❏
Day 6	Covenant Meditation on 2 Corinthians 4:7-12	God will rescue us.	❏
Day 7	Group Meeting Experience with 1 Corinthians 13:4-8	Love never fails.	❏

Episode 8

Day 1	Deuteronomy 5–9	The Ten Commandments and the greatest commandment	❏
Day 2	Deuteronomy 29–32	Old and new covenants	❏
Day 3	Joshua 1–2; 23–24	Moses reinvented	❏
Day 4	Judges 1–2; 19–21	Downward spiral	❏
Day 5	1 Samuel 13–15; 28:3-25	Tragedy of King Saul	❏
Day 6	Covenant Meditation on Deuteronomy 6:4-9	Renewing the covenant	❏
Day 7	Group Meeting Experience with Deuteronomy 6:1-19	A portrait of the covenant	❏

Old Testament

Book of the Bible	Abbreviation	Episode	Participant Guide Page
Genesis	Gen	2	Creating, 21
Exodus	Exod	3	Creating, 31
Leviticus	Lev	3	Creating, 31
Numbers	Num	3	Creating, 31
Deuteronomy	Deut	8	Creating, 83
Joshua	Josh	8	Creating, 83
Judges	Judg	8	Creating, 83
Ruth	Ruth	9	Living, 9
1 Samuel	1 Sam	8	Creating, 83
2 Samuel	2 Sam	11	Living, 33
1 Kings	1 Kgs	11	Living, 33
2 Kings	2 Kgs	11	Living, 33
1 Chronicles	1 Chron	22	Trusting, 65
2 Chronicles	2 Chron	22	Trusting, 65
Ezra	Ezra	22	Trusting, 65
Nehemiah	Neh	22	Trusting, 65
Esther	Esth	9	Living, 9
Job	Job	19	Trusting, 31
Psalms	Ps	18	Trusting, 21
Proverbs	Prov	13	Living, 55
Ecclesiastes	Eccl	13	Living, 55
Song of Songs	Song	9	Living, 9
Isaiah	Isa	16 21	Living, 85 Trusting, 53
Jeremiah	Jer	20	Trusting, 41
Lamentations	Lam	20	Trusting, 41
Ezekiel	Ezek	20	Trusting, 41
Daniel	Dan	23	Trusting, 75
Hosea	Hos	16	Living, 85
Joel	Joel	16	Living, 85
Amos	Amos	16	Living, 85
Obadiah	Obad	16	Living, 85
Jonah	Jon	16	Living, 85
Micah	Mic	16	Living, 85
Nahum	Nah	16	Living, 85
Habakkuk	Hab	16	Living, 85
Zephaniah	Zeph	16	Living, 85
Haggai	Hag	16	Living, 85
Zechariah	Zech	16	Living, 85
Malachi	Mal	16	Living, 85

New Testament

Book of the Bible	Abbreviation	Episode	Participant Guide Page
Matthew	Matt	4	Creating, 41
Mark	Mark	4	Creating, 41
Luke	Luke	10	Living, 21
John	John	17	Trusting, 9
Acts	Acts	10	Living, 21
Romans	Rom	5	Creating, 51
1 Corinthians	1 Cor	7	Creating, 71
2 Corinthians	2 Cor	7	Creating, 71
Galatians	Gal	5	Creating, 51
Ephesians	Eph	14	Living, 65
Philippians	Phil	14	Living, 65
Colossians	Col	14	Living, 65
1 Thessalonians	1 Thess	12	Living, 43
2 Thessalonians	2 Thess	12	Living, 43
1 Timothy	1 Tim	12	Living, 43
2 Timothy	2 Tim	12	Living, 43
Titus	Titus	12	Living, 43
Philemon	Phlm	14	Living, 65
Hebrews	Heb	6	Creating, 63
James	Jas	15	Living, 75
1 Peter	1 Pet	15	Living, 75
2 Peter	2 Pet	15	Living, 75
1 John	1 John	17	Trusting, 9
2 John	2 John	17	Trusting, 9
3 John	3 John	17	Trusting, 9
Jude	Jude	15	Living, 75
Revelation	Rev	24	Trusting, 85

CREATING
the covenant

Covenant Creative Team

Editorial

Theodore Hiebert, Old Testament Editor

Jaime Clark-Soles, New Testament Editor

Magrey deVega, Leadership Editor

Pam Hawkins, Meditations Editor

David Teel, Project Manager

Paul Franklyn, General Editor and Associate Publisher

Neil M. Alexander, Publisher

Video Cohosts

Christine Chakoian, Senior Pastor,
    First Presbyterian Church, Lake Forest, IL

Shane Stanford, Senior Pastor,
    Christ United Methodist Church, Memphis, TN

Writers: Creating the Covenant

Episode 2	Theodore Hiebert, Francis A. McGaw Professor of Old Testament, McCormick Theological Seminary, Chicago, IL
Episode 3	Alejandro F. Botta, Associate Professor of Hebrew Bible, Boston University, Boston, MA
Episode 4	Stephanie B. Crowder, Adjunct Professor of Biblical Studies, McCormick Theological Seminary, Chicago, IL
Episode 5	Diane Grace Chen, Associate Professor of New Testament, Palmer Theological Seminary, King of Prussia, PA
Episode 6	David A. deSilva, Trustees' Distinguished Professor of New Testament and Greek, Ashland Theological Seminary, Ashland, OH
Episode 7	Monya A. Stubbs, Former Associate Professor of New Testament, Austin Presbyterian Theological Seminary, Austin, TX
Episode 8	Brent A. Strawn, Professor of Old Testament, Candler School of Theology, Atlanta, GA

Production and Design

Christy Lynch, Production Editor

Jeff Moore, Packaging and Interior Design

Emily Keafer, Interior Design

PerfecType, Typesetting

Robert Dupuy, Covenant App Developer

CovenantBibleStudy.com

Christie Durand, Analyst

Gregory Davis, Developer

David Burns, Designer

Dan Heile, Database Analyst

Video Production: Revolution Pictures, Inc.

Randy Brewer, Executive Producer

Michelle Abnet, Producer

Ry Cox, Codirector

Jeff Venable, Codirector

Chris Adams, Photography Director

Brandon Eller, Prop Master

Dave Donnelly, Post Editor

Perry Trest, Colorist

Creating the Covenant

RELATIONSHIPS
Reading the Bible to live and love well

Covenant Prayer

For those who want to learn how to love God and others

They read aloud from the scroll, the Instruction from God, explaining and interpreting it so the people could understand what they heard. (Nehemiah 8:8)

For those whom God makes new

This day is holy to our Lord. Don't be sad, because the joy from the Lord is your strength! (Nehemiah 8:10)

OUR LONGING FOR RELATIONSHIP

Covenant names our yearning to live and belong in loving relationships with self, God, and others.

LIFE THAT FITS AND CONNECTS

We probably have seen scrapbooks or family photo albums (in binders, books, or online). What kind of pictures or mementos do you find in books like this? Did your family keep a scrapbook or photo album from your childhood?

Covenant Bible Study promises new life that fits and connects with God and others. Life that makes sense. Life that finds its source in God. Life lived together.

The Bible is a book like no other, and reading it is a rewarding experience. The assumption is that reading the Bible will improve our lives. But in spite of this assumption, many of us try to read this book and give up—usually after trying to read it from cover to cover. We often become confused by the strange names, places, and events that seem so distant from our daily lives. It can make us feel defeated, and so we throw in the towel and trust that someone else (pastor, scholar, or teacher) will make sense of this book and pass on the "high points" to the rest of us.

But our anxiety about reading the Bible may be connected to a deeper frustration and longing—a longing to connect with and come alive to something real, something lasting that promises to help us live well. Awash in a world of flickering words and images on glowing screens, we thirst for depth, for something that faithfully delivers on a promise to make a difference where we learn, work, and play. We want more than a superficial faith. Yet for many, the Bible seems like the last place for this kind of reality check.

Covenant Bible Study is one way to dispel this anxiety and reconnect with the deepest realities of our faith. Its goal is to cultivate lifelong trust in God and help participants discover the Bible as a friend for life. Covenant is based on the simple idea that we live well when we love well. When we read it together, we remember and retell the deepest story we know. This is the story of who we are, where we come from, and where we go wrong. And the story ends well because faithful love is at work in everything to restore hope, freedom, and wholeness to our lives.

The Bible follows the sometimes faithful and sometimes faithless responses of Israel and the church, tracking changes in the lives of key people and the community itself as they respond to God's call. We find ourselves in tales of rivalry and rebellion, and in stories of corruption, catastrophe, and crisis. We see our own anxious desire for security expressed in its narratives of idolatry and rigid tribal boundaries. But we also see our misplaced loyalties graced by God's restoring love. These grace-filled stories give us hope that God will make beautiful things out of the fragments and dust of our fallen lives.

The Bible speaks in more than one voice. It contains many conversations and perspectives, inviting us to join a discussion that began with creation in Genesis and extends to our street corners, coffee shops, offices, schools, and dinner tables. Covenant Bible Study is one way to continue that conversation. When we ask questions, share stories, and wrestle with some of the biggest issues facing us as human beings, this living conversation is woven into our lives. Reading the Bible together helps us deal with questions like, "How—or even—*Is* God with us? Is any of this real or true?" Real experiences and real questions come together in our search for something we can trust—a scripture reliable enough to be called a friend for life.

In the process, we discover that God is not anxious about this ongoing discussion, but that God actually shows up in some powerful ways, in loyal relationship, when we open ourselves and risk joining the conversation. Covenant Bible Study is an opportunity to belong to a group of friends discovering how the Bible is a companion for life.

Do your parents or grandparents ever tell competing versions of the same events? Do you have any "memories" that turned out to be the story you've always been told? Does that make them more or less reliable?

A Covenant Bible Study consists of:

1. A **small group** of adults who pledge to read and study the Bible individually and together for an extended period of time. The group's purpose is to deepen commitment to live as faithful followers of Jesus Christ.

2. An **experience** that trains participants in disciplined daily Bible reading, prayer, and holy conversation. Participants learn these skills by responding to participant guides, study Bibles, videos, and devotional meditations. The experience becomes accountable at weekly meetings in a group setting for fellowship, learning, and the shared practice of interpreting scripture. This setting is where scripture meets everyday experience within and beyond your church life.

3. A **promise** to cultivate practical wisdom, so that the knowledge of the participant and the group is enlarged when interpreting the Bible and conversing about life. What results is a covenant relationship with God that will redeem a broken world in need of transformation.

The Bible is a conversation partner for life. Reading it recalls and even rewrites our deepest stories, helping us recognize and respond to the true God who saves a suffering, shattered world.

The Covenant Bible experience helps participants:

1. **learn** by dispelling anxiety about understanding the Bible;

2. **grow** by practicing conversation about scripture and relationships in a group;

3. **change** by improving skills for reading the Bible and living faithfully;

4. **discover** by naming your unique identity and purpose through the scriptural witness;

5. **share** by belonging to a group of friends in faith;

6. **experience** by invoking God's power and presence through spiritual reading and listening practices; and

7. **serve** by responding to what you learn and bringing covenant love to others.

Living well depends primarily on the attachments that we form. These bonds can be described in terms of who and what we love. Who and what we love expresses who we are (our identity) and also shows what matters most to each of us (our purpose).

In the Old Testament, Deuteronomy insists that the basic human yearning for healthy relationship is based in faithful love: "Israel, listen! Our God is the LORD! Only the LORD! Love the LORD your God with all your heart, all your being, and all your strength" (Deut 6:4-5). In the New Testament, Jesus acknowledges Deuteronomy ("love the Lord your God") as the greatest expectation in the scriptures, and then he preaches: "You must love your neighbor as you love yourself" (Matt 22:39). Jesus confirms that you will find it hard to love a neighbor if your well-being (your whole heart and mind) is fragmented or distracted by substitutes for loyal love or by selfish desires.

Love has a learning curve. When we better understand God's faithful love expressed through scripture in the stories, songs, instructions, prophecies, and prayers for help, we find that living well together is always about our relationships.

Covenant as an organizing pattern for studying the whole scripture

"Covenant" is the solemn and enduring commitment made between God and human beings to be in a fruitful and creative relationship. When Christians speak about a relationship with God, we invoke the language and images of covenant. To express the relationship, we might say, "God is my father," or "Jesus is my friend," or "I am God's child." These expressions invoke commitment and loyalty.

This emphasis on covenant in the Bible is one way to get the big picture. It helps make sense of a long, ancient book that seems very strange and overwhelming. The Christian Bible is actually a library of sixty-six interrelated books. Think of the Bible as a quilt with sixty-six squares. Covenant is a dominant pattern that runs through this quilt because:

1. In the Torah (Genesis through Deuteronomy), God's relationship with God's people is grounded in a series of covenants. Torah is the Instruction (or Teaching; also called "the Law" in the King James Version) that maintains the relationship between God's word (the expectations established by God) and God's faithful or loyal people. The Torah shows that what we put in our mouths and consume with our minds will affect our well-being, the health of our relationship with God, and our relationships with others. As you will learn in Episode 2 on the Torah and Genesis, covenant in the Bible is based on the relationships formed by the first human families. Our best (and sometimes most painful) experiences in life come from learning how to love each other in a family.

2. Sometimes covenant is also understood in contractual and legal terms. We use the word *covenant* when describing how a group of neighbors might agree to get along with each other for mutual benefit. This sort of "neighborhood agreement" goes back to ancient times, when a tribal leader or ruler would "cut a covenant" with a neighboring tribe. These legal analogies can stimulate useful conversation about the responsibilities that are embedded in contemporary relationships with our families, friends, and government. However, the legal sanctions

The Christian Bible is actually a library of sixty-six interrelated books. Think of the Bible as a quilt with sixty-six squares. Covenant is a dominant pattern that runs through this quilt.

and retributions that were prescribed for violating a covenant in ancient societies can raise difficult issues that require thoughtful Christian reflection. A Covenant Bible Study group is a safe place to discuss the expectations we have for each other in our homes and communities.

3. Covenant is the dominant theme of the core stories (about the leading personalities) in the Bible, including the five major covenants that are based in promises and fulfilled through Noah, Abraham, Moses, David, and Jesus. A story is a great way to show us (rather than simply tell us) what faithful love looks like. The books of Esther and Ruth, for example, are models of faithful covenant love. The history writings from Deuteronomy through 2 Kings are also based in covenants that show how the well-being of God's people is determined by their loyalty to God and their commitment to this relationship.

4. Many of the prophets, but especially Hosea and Jeremiah, are schooled by covenant theology as they confront leaders who have responsibilities toward God and their communities. A breached covenant is how the prophets eventually explain the exile and the near extermination or scattering of Israelites by Babylon and Assyria. Jeremiah, in the "Book of the Covenant" (Jer 30–33), yearns for a new covenant that is cut into our hearts.

5. We look back at that expectation and yearning for a covenant inscribed on our hearts, and we as Christians realize that this new life is possible through Jesus, the one who reconciles us to God through his faithfulness on the cross. In the Gospels, God's kingdom is a vision of a better future for the new community of Christ-followers.

6. When the early Christians were "born again" and referred to each other as "sister" or "brother," they established their kinship through a family. Covenant life was the context for the letters to the Christian communities (for example, at Corinth or Ephesus) as they grappled with the ethical implications of living in relationships. This kind of covenant community is apparent when referring to Jesus as the head and the church as the body. This is also why Paul often refers to himself as the father of his parishioners. When we think of the most intimate relationships known to human beings—mother, father, sister, brother, lover, child, partner, spouse, friend—each of these identities was and is used by Christians to describe the covenant relationships between the people, their Lord, and their community.

Many Christians make a promise to read the whole Bible in a year. That is really hard to do, especially alone. Most people stall before Leviticus. To gain an in-depth understanding of the whole Bible, Covenant offers patient and flexible guidance. The three participant guides encourage your group to meet in eight-week segments:

1. *Creating the Covenant*

2. *Living the Covenant*

3. *Trusting the Covenant*

It feels great each time your group finishes working through one of the participant guides, because it means you've also finished working through about a third of the Bible. The books of the Bible are arranged to cover the whole scripture while emphasizing the themes that are drawn from the covenants in the Bible.

The initial eight weeks feature how the covenant community is created and established. The next eight weeks feature how the community wisely lives out their covenant in faithful love. The final eight weeks feature how the community and individuals are restored to hope—to trust God when troubling things happen.

Because the Christian Bible is fixed in a certain order from Genesis to Revelation, people often try to study scripture in that order. Typically Christians end up neglecting the unfamiliar Old Testament books and sticking to the New Testament (and perhaps some of the Psalms). While it might seem surprising to mix the books of the Old Testament and the New Testament, this Bible study's three-part covenant pattern will help us see that the New Testament writers were in conversation with the covenant themes of the Old Testament books.

Loving others in your group

Holy conversation about the Bible is vital to your spiritual health. You are part of a Covenant group. In a group, the participants get more than knowledge about the Bible. Knowledge isn't enough to sustain or deepen trust in God. Group participants actually form covenant relationships with each other as they examine and practice what it means to stay in love with God. As you learn to share and love and serve together, the members of the Covenant group make a commitment to each other. They learn to forgive each other if offended, and they make a commitment together to deepen their relationship with God.

Your leader will convene the Covenant group each week and help you develop a transforming conversation about the scriptures. This conversational approach is modeled for you in the weekly video episodes about the books you are studying. The Bible is most transformative when it is read and discussed together. Your understanding and life experience is shared, and as you listen to another's understanding of the story or hear about their practical experience, God's presence (the Holy Spirit) begins to turn and change hearts and minds. Amazing hope suddenly seems possible because God's love is discovered through these personal relationships.

Resources for the Covenant experience

1. *Participant Guides:* The three Covenant participant guides show you what to read and offer space to interact personally with the daily Bible readings, the prayers, and the weekly Covenant Meditations. The guides are available from Cokesbury as a print set (or individually); or as enhanced eBooks in the Covenant Bible Study app (iOS and Android) for tablets and personal computers. The app is available from iTunes and Google Play.

2. *Covenant Meditations:* Many participants find great personal benefit and contentment in an intimate connection with God through praying scripture. In addition to the once-weekly meditation in the participant guides (on Day 6), a set of sixty-six additional Covenant meditations is available in print or as an eBook.

3. *CEB Study Bible:* Participants and leaders are encouraged to obtain and use this study Bible (published in 2013) to inform the daily readings and the group meeting experiences for Covenant. The *CEB Study Bible* is available in print, and it is also an option for purchase within the Covenant Bible Study app.

4. *CovenantBibleStudy.com:* Encourage your leader to collect everyone's e-mail address and register your group online. In addition to meeting reminders, benefits include a daily e-mail of the assigned Bible reading to everyone in the group. You can also visit online stores such as iTunes and Google Play to download the daily Bible readings as a navigable MP3 audiobook, based on the enhanced audio edition of the Common English Bible. At the website, participants can also download or stream the weekly video episodes (for a small fee), perhaps for a weekly meeting that was missed or to see what is ahead in the next weekly episode. Additional videos (including Bible stories retold) are mentioned occasionally in the text of the participant guides. These are also located at the website for personal or group viewing.

Guidelines for reading the Bible

Covenant is explained above as the key pattern throughout this in-depth Bible study. However, many participants will come to the Bible with further questions about how we got the Bible, when the stories or writing of the Bible took place, why we have an Old Testament and a New Testament, or who decided that we should read the Bible. These questions are answered in the articles of the *CEB Study Bible*. When you feel lost, get your bearings from the following articles, cited by page number and found toward the end of the *CEB Study Bible* (after the book of Revelation and before the phrase concordance):

You can find more Bible study resources with the Covenant smartphone/tablet app or by visiting CovenantBibleStudy.com.

Next week in Episode 2, we will start with a fundamental human question: Who are we? In Genesis and the rest of the Torah, we learn about creating covenants with God and others. You will encounter God's covenant with all creation and then God's particular covenant with the people who descended from Abraham and Sarah.

SIGNS OF FAITHFUL LOVE

Covenant people read the Bible together to learn how to love God and others better.

Torah: Genesis

WHO ARE WE?
Creating covenants with God and others

Bible Readings

Day 1: Genesis 1–3

Day 2: Genesis 6:5–9:17; 11:1-9

Day 3: Genesis 12; 15; 17; 22

Day 4: Genesis 27–28; 32–33

Day 5: Genesis 37; 41; 43; 45; 50

Day 6: Covenant Meditation on Genesis 1:26-31

Day 7: Group Meeting Experience with Genesis 9:7-17

Covenant Prayer

For those who are suffering in chaos

Hear my prayer, LORD! Listen closely to my cry for help! (Psalm 39:12)

For those who celebrate new creation

Your word gives me new life. (Psalm 119:50)

OUR LONGING FOR RELATIONSHIP

We get into trouble—hurting ourselves, those we love, and the world—when we forget who we are and to whom we belong.

TORAH

The Christian and Jewish communities consider the first five books of the Bible as a separate portion of scripture. Christians call these books the Pentateuch, or "five books." The books tell stories about the earliest events in God's relationship with God's people. Jews call these books the Torah, which the Common English Bible translates as "Instruction." Beginning with the King James Version, however, *Torah* was often translated as "the Law." By calling these books the Torah, our attention is focused on the great covenant God made with the Israelites at Mount Sinai—described in Exodus, Leviticus, Numbers, and Deuteronomy. The Torah presents the instructions or teaching for worshipping God and living in a covenant community.

The aim of the Torah is to answer the question, "Who are we?" and the answer is vast and all-encompassing. Torah explains not only the unique character of the people of Israel and of God's relationship to the people, but also their role in the larger world. To do this, the Torah explains the nature of humanity in all of its cultural diversity. The Torah also explains God's relationship to Israel, and even more broadly, God's relationship to the created world in which Israel lived. The Torah's authors do all of this by telling the story of their own past, of how God brought nature, humanity, and Israel itself into being at the very beginning of time.

The Torah story is structured around crucial, community-shaping events. It begins with the creation of the natural world and the human role within it, followed by the first age of history, in which the human community fell into violence and perished in the great flood (Gen 1–8). In the new era of history following the flood, three great covenants redefine the human community and the role of the people of Israel within it.

> **Optional:** *An additional video on the tower of Babel and the unique role of Israel is available for download from* **CovenantBibleStudy.com**.

The first is God's covenant with Noah, humanity, and all living things (Gen 9:1-17). The second is God's covenant with Abraham and with his descendants, by which God selects a particular line of humanity for a particular role within it (Gen 15; 17). And the third is God's covenant with Israel itself, the descendants of Jacob's twelve sons, at Mount Sinai (Exod 19; 24; 31), where the great

---

The Torah presents the instructions or teaching for worshipping God and living in a covenant community.

In the new era of history following the flood, three great covenants redefine the human community and the role of the people of Israel within it.

22

body of instructions that would define Israel as a community were collected and recorded.

The Torah, like many books in the Old Testament, and like the Old Testament as a whole, is the product of multiple voices from ancient Israel. Jewish and Christian traditions eventually came to regard the entire Pentateuch as transcribed by a single individual Moses, but biblical scholars in recent centuries have noticed evidence of multiple authors: double accounts of the same event, contrasting styles and theological perspectives, and knowledge of events later than Moses' time.

The liveliest stories in Genesis, Exodus, and Numbers come from the Torah's two earliest authors, who both lived during the Israelite monarchy: the Yahwist, so named because he used God's personal name, Yahweh (rendered "the LORD" in the CEB); and the Elohist, so named because he used the common word for "God," *Elohim*, in his narrative. The third contributor, a Priestly Writer, added his own traditions to the Yahwist's and Elohist's stories and organized them around God's three great covenants with Noah, Abraham, and Israel. He also contributed most of the expectations and instructions related to the Sinai covenant in Exodus, Leviticus, and Numbers. The fourth contributor's work, the book of Deuteronomy, was included in the Torah because it provided another record of the Sinai covenant. But based on style, theology, and vocabulary, we can tell that it was originally intended as the introduction to the Historical Books (Joshua through 2 Kings) that follow it. For this reason, it has been placed with the Historical Books in Episode 8.

GENESIS

The book of Genesis tells the first two parts of the larger Torah story: (1) how the world came into being and what role Israel's ancestors were given within it; and (2) how Israel itself emerged as a distinct community within the human race.

The first part of this story is described especially in the creation narratives at the beginning of Genesis (Gen 1–3). The authors of Genesis describe who they are in relation to the natural world, which they inhabit. In these creation stories they show themselves not merely as members of the Israelite community, or even of the human community, but also as members of the larger community of life in the entire creation, within which they are given clear roles and responsibilities. These roles and responsibilities reflect Israel's

The stories of Israel's origins and identity are family stories.

own understanding of its connection with nature and its place in the particular landscape and environment it inhabited.

In the second part of this Torah story in Genesis, when the new world is re-created after the flood, the authors of Genesis explain who they are in relation to the larger world of human cultures that they inhabit. To do this, they employ a complex web of genealogies with family stories to accompany them. These genealogies provide a comprehensive cultural map that documents how all of the peoples descended from the single family of Noah. This map shows how the different peoples are related to each other within the cultural world experienced by the authors of Genesis, and where exactly Israel fits into this larger human family.

In these genealogies and family stories, the main characters stand not only for themselves but for the people who descended from them and who made up the nations with which the authors of Genesis were familiar. Jacob and Esau, for example, in this week's reading for Day 4 (Gen 27–28; 32–33), represent the brothers in a family, but also the nations of Israel and Edom that descended from them.

In the stories of Genesis, community is conceived in terms of family and kinship systems. The stories of Israel's origins and identity are family stories, largely because the family is its basic unit. Its families are grouped into clans, its clans into tribes, and its tribes into a people, the nation of Israel. The authors thought carefully about their relationships in terms of the privileges and responsibilities of kinship. They examined Israel's relationship to God and its covenants with God, Israel's relationship to other cultures, and the family, clan, and tribal relationships within Israel itself. This kinship culture had consequences for entering into covenants and building community.

Day 1: Genesis 1–3
Creation and the human role within it

The Bible begins its account of who Israel was as God's people by describing who they were in relation to their environment, the world of nature that surrounded and sustained them. By starting their story at the creation of the world, the biblical authors affirm that the first and most basic community of life is the entire natural world.

Genesis actually preserves two traditions about the world's beginnings and Israel's place within it. Both of these traditions view the world from Israel's ancient understandings of the world and their particular geographical location within it—not from the new knowledge of the cosmos gained by modern science.

The first creation tradition (Gen 1:1–2:4*a*, probably from the Priestly Writer) describes creation in seven days. This description establishes the Sabbath on the seventh day as part of the world's own rhythms and orders. It's written in a very orderly style that may have been intended for reading in a worship setting. It gives humans a high role in creation: We are made in God's own image and commissioned to take charge of the animal world. The second creation tradition (Gen 2:4*b*–3:24, and probably from the Yahwist, who uses the divine name Yahweh) describes creation in a small, local garden. It's more earthy and is written in a more informal, story-like style. And it gives humans a much more modest role in creation: They are made out of the earth's topsoil and commissioned to farm (or "serve") the fertile land from which they were created.

As you read these two creation stories, note their similarities and differences and consider how more than one perspective provides a deeper understanding of the world and humanity than a single account could.

Day 2: Genesis 6:5–9:17; 11:1-9
End of the old world—beginning of the new world

Biblical writers shared the common ancient idea that a great flood brought an end to the first age of human history and introduced the new age of history in which they themselves lived. In these ancient stories, something went wrong in the first age that required starting over. Humanity had become violent and corrupt. So God selected Noah, the moral and exemplary man of his time, together with his family and a pair from each species of animal, to survive the flood and begin the world anew.

God begins the new world by establishing a covenant relationship with all living things. The covenant offers them life, protection, and a relationship with God for all time (Gen 9:1-17). Included in the Bible's first covenant are the entire human race descended from Noah's family and all of the living things who survived the flood. The story of the city of Babel that follows (Gen 11:1-9) explains how the human members of God's first covenant became culturally diverse, even though they descended from a single family and wished to preserve a single culture. Because some readers have misread the story of Babel as a story of human pride and God's punishment for it, they have claimed that God rejected God's covenant relationship with the human race in order to make a covenant with Abraham alone. This biblical story, however, tells us that God's covenant with Abraham was a particular covenant within God's larger covenant with the human race as a whole.

What feelings do you have about cultural and racial differences in your neighborhood? In your church?

Day 3: Genesis 12; 15; 17; 22
Abraham and nationhood

God's covenant with Abraham is the Bible's second covenant, preserved by the Yahwist (Gen 15) and the Priestly Writer (Gen 17). It shows that within God's larger covenant with all of humanity and all living things (Gen 9:1-17), God established a particular kind of relationship with this line of Noah's descendants. This relationship is one that will define the people of Israel as a unique community within the human race as a whole. That community will be established as a nation among other ancient nations (Gen 12:2; 17:6), with a flourishing population (Gen 15:5; 17:2), and a land to sustain them (Gen 12:7; 15:18).

> **Optional:** *An additional video retelling the story of Abraham, Sarah, and the three visitors is available for download from* **CovenantBibleStudy.com**.

This model of a community in covenant relationship with God is based in kinship, culture, and politics. It mirrors the religious life and practices of its time and place, when culture, politics, and religion were a single integrated system. It contains a number of powerful ideas that sustained the lives of these people: the confidence in an enduring relationship with God, the belief that their lives and identities played an important part in God's world, a strong national and communal solidarity, and a close relationship to the land. At the same time, this model of community is packaged with specific cultural, ethnic, patriarchal, and political aspects that contemporary Christians may no longer wish to define in their own communities.

Both the Yahwist and the Priestly Writer have preserved records of the covenant with Abraham. Compare the Yahwist's style and theology of covenant in Genesis 15 with the style and theology of his creation story (Gen 2:4b–3:24). Compare the Priestly Writer's style and theology of covenant in Genesis 17 with the style and theology of his creation story (Gen 1:1–2:4a) and his record of the covenant with Noah (Gen 9:1-17).

Compare the covenant story in Genesis 15 with the covenant story in Genesis 17.

Day 4: Genesis 27–28; 32–33
Jacob and the biblical family

While Abraham is Israel's most typical ancestor to whom the promises of nationhood were first made, Jacob, his grandson, is the ancestor who received the nation's name, Israel, and whose twelve sons became ancestors of the twelve tribes that made up the nation (Gen 29–30). These stories about Jacob explain how he, rather than his older brother, Esau, became Isaac's primary heir, and they reveal traits of biblical characters and their families that puzzle and trouble modern readers. Jacob, Israel's namesake, and his mother, Rebekah, had to deceive Isaac and Esau to acquire the blessing that God gave to Jacob.

Community in ancient Israel, as in these stories of its ancestors, is grounded in family structures. These structures privilege the oldest male member of the family, the patriarch, and his oldest son, the family's legal heir. These same structures exclude women and secondary sons from the status and agency to participate in family decisions and to carry on the family's legacy. Rebekah and Jacob find ways to subvert traditional structures in order to claim their voices and their places in the family. Against convention and cultural expectations, God sides in each generation in the book of Genesis with those excluded from power and privilege within these kinship systems. The story of Rebekah and Jacob is one example of this (Gen 25:21-23; 28:13-15).

What puzzles or troubles you in the family stories about Jacob and Rebekah?

Day 5: Genesis 37; 41; 43; 45; 50
Joseph and his brothers in Egypt

The stories about Jacob's sons that conclude Genesis are some of the most colorful and emotional in the book. A key theme in them, as in every family story in Genesis, is sibling rivalry. As the first and most basic conflict in life, sibling rivalry in Genesis represents the conflicts that arise not just in the family, but also within the larger community of Israel, and even between Israel and its neighboring nations. The conflicts between Jacob's sons also represent the conflicts between the later tribes made up of their descendants, just as the conflict between Jacob and Esau also represents in a larger scope the conflict between their descendants, the Israelites and the Edomites.

In every family in Genesis but one, this deep and primal conflict that threatened to tear apart the fabric of the community was resolved through generosity and a great capacity for understanding. The one exception is the family who lived in the troubled age before the flood when Cain killed his brother, Abel (Gen 4:1-16). In all of the other family dramas, bloodshed was averted. In the stories of Jacob and Esau and of Joseph and his brothers, the wronged brother, with good reason and enough power to take revenge, instead forgave and restored the relationship that was broken.

The other key theme in these concluding stories in Genesis is God's protection of Jacob's family from death by famine. This protection extended beyond Jacob's family, however, to include all of Egypt and all of the known world that came to buy grain (Gen 41:57; 45:5). Before Egypt became a furnace of oppression in Exodus through Numbers, it was a refuge from hunger that shared its bounty with the world.

How did Jacob's troubled family resolve their conflicts?

Day 6: Genesis 1:26-31
Covenant Meditation: Who are we?

Each week on Day 6, we will approach and encounter scripture in a different way than in our study on Days 1–5. Through the following exercise, we will practice one form of spiritual reading that has been taught in the church for many generations—the practice of using our imagination. This practice is designed to deepen our ability to listen for what God is trying to reveal to us through scripture. It represents one way that we can learn to read the Bible devotionally, while also participating in study of the texts.

Read Genesis 1:26-31 again, but do so slowly, paying attention to each word, phrase, and action. In this passage, God addresses our question, "Who are we?" even before humanity is added to the scene of creation. Notice that what God says, God then does, and that we as human beings take form in God's imagination and words before we become part of the created order on earth.

Now read these verses of Genesis once more, using your imagination to place yourself nearby as God speaks and creates. What do you see? What colors, shapes, animals, and movements? What do you hear? What sounds come to mind as you read these words? Are there aromas or scents that you might associate with this scene as you take your time reading: the scent of the earth, of water, of animals? Can you imagine the feel of any textures, objects, or movements: breeze, rain, dirt? Allow all of your senses to bring your imagination to bear on this passage in Genesis, and notice what is stirred up for you. If you would like, write down your reflections as you follow this practice of spiritual reading, and then look back over how this way of reading may have opened the passage to you in a new way.

Group Meeting Experience

Genesis 9:7-17 | The Bible's first covenant

At the beginning of the new world following the flood, God makes the covenant that becomes the foundation for the Torah covenants that follow: the covenants with Abraham and with the people of Israel at Mount Sinai.

1. To gain an appreciation for the style of the Priestly Writer who structured the Torah around three great covenants, compare the language, vocabulary, and style of this covenant with the covenants with Abraham in Genesis 17 and with Israel in Exodus 31:12-18. Also compare to these the Priestly account of the world's creation in seven days in Genesis 1:1–2:4a. What are the key words, phrases, and features of Priestly style and thought?

2. With whom does God enter into relationship in this covenant?

3. What does this covenant claim about God's relationship to the world as a whole?

4. The Priestly Writer probably lived during the time of the exile (after 587 BCE), when his people's past had been destroyed and their future was in doubt. In this context, how might such a covenant provide hope for survival and a way forward?

5. In the Bible's first covenant, how might God's relation to the world, to all its forms of life, and to all its people inform our own understanding of our place and role in the world?

SIGNS OF FAITHFUL LOVE

God's covenant with us returns us to our true selves—made in the image of God—and sends the Covenant people out to be a blessing to the world God loves.

Exodus, Leviticus, Numbers

FREEDOM AND INSTRUCTION
Privileges and responsibilities of the covenant

Bible Readings

Day 1: Exodus 1–4

Day 2: Exodus 13:17–15:21

Day 3: Exodus 20–24

Day 4: Leviticus 19–22

Day 5: Numbers 11–14

Day 6: Covenant Meditation on Leviticus 19:1-2

Day 7: Group Meeting Experience with Exodus 20:1-17

Covenant Prayer

For children in refugee camps, war zones, sweatshops, and other oppressive circumstances where they are not free to receive a formal education

I will bless the LORD who advises me; even at night I am instructed in the depths of my mind. (Psalm 16:7)

For those who follow the call to teach, instruct, and share God's wisdom with children and youth

I will instruct you and teach you about the direction you should go. I'll advise you and keep my eye on you. (Psalm 32:8)

OUR LONGING FOR RELATIONSHIP

It's a privilege and a gift to experience a committed relationship, but a lasting relationship is always confirmed through responsibilities and expectations.

FREEDOM

Israel's liberation from oppression in Egypt, their journey through the wilderness, and their possession of the promised land is a story that echoes throughout the Old and the New Testaments.

Notice that God promises the land to Abraham (Gen 15:7), then to Isaac (Gen 26:3), and then to Jacob (Gen 28:13), without any of them ever receiving it. It's only after the Israelites cry out from their oppression that God notices and "remembers" the promise God made to Israel's ancestors (Exod 2:23-24). This triggers God's saving action. The first lesson from this liberation story is, therefore, that no liberation begins unless there is a strong outcry by the oppressed (compare Neh 5:1). No people can really be rescued unless they become aware of their need for help (compare Mark 2:17).

God's response to the people isn't timid. God states, "I am the LORD. I'll bring you out from Egyptian forced labor. I'll rescue you from your slavery to them. I'll set you free with great power and with momentous events of justice" (Exod 6:6). The same verbs are used in the New Testament to describe God's salvation (compare Luke 24:21; Matt 6:13; Col 1:13). This liberation of Israel was a very political act that became symbolic of how God can reverse human circumstances.

Several traditions are brought together in Exodus, Leviticus, and Numbers, resulting in the story of liberation as we have it in the Bible today (see the introduction to Genesis). The final editor was successful in combining all of them into a coherent narrative, but some inconsistencies and alternative versions of the same event still remain in the final form of the story. Examples of these different traditions can be found in the accounts of Moses and his father-in-law from Exodus 18 (Elohist) and Numbers 10:29-32 (Yahwist); the complaints of the Israelites in Exodus 16:1-12 (Priestly Writer) and Numbers 11:1-6 (Elohist); the manna from Exodus 16:13-35 (Priestly Writer) and Numbers 11:7-35 (Elohist); and the accounts of the crossing of the sea in Exodus 15.

The exodus tradition, hundreds of years later in Israelite history, served as a theological framework for the liberation from Babylon and return to Israel's homeland after the exile. God made proclamations to the exilic community full of images from the exodus:

The LORD your redeemer, the holy one of Israel, says,
For your sake, I have sent an army to Babylon,
and brought down all the bars,

turning the Chaldeans' singing into a lament.
I am the LORD, your holy one, Israel's creator, your king!
The LORD says—who makes a way in the sea
   and a path in the mighty waters,
   who brings out chariot and horse, army and battalion;
   they will lie down together and will not rise;
   they will be extinguished, extinguished like a wick.
Don't remember the prior things;
   don't ponder ancient history.
Look! I'm doing a new thing;
   now it sprouts up; don't you recognize it?
I'm making a way in the desert,
   paths in the wilderness. (Isa 43:14-19)

Both acts of salvation, the liberation from Egypt and the liberation from Babylon, were fulfilled when the Israelites returned to live freely in the land of Israel.

The exodus tradition, hundreds of years later in Israelite history, served as a theological framework for the liberation from Babylon and return to Israel's homeland after the exile.

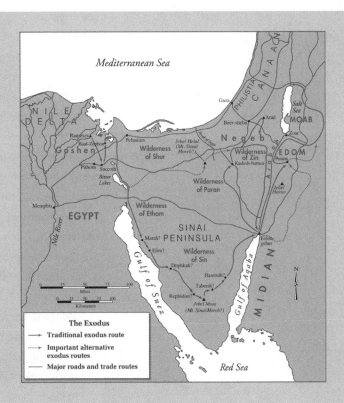

INSTRUCTION

The main purpose of the Torah is to teach the Israelites how to live a holy life in the midst of a just society. Such emphasis on the right behavior is also well represented in the New Testament, especially in the letter from James. Matthew (a very Jewish Gospel) also highlights this responsibility when Jesus states that "only those who do the will of my Father" will enter the kingdom of heaven (Matt 7:21).

Notice that the Instruction in the books of Exodus, Leviticus, and Numbers contains almost no statement or list of beliefs. Instead they include a long (perhaps today we would say too long) list of precepts, commandments, and ordinances for teaching Israel how to live an abundant, fulfilling, holy life (Lev 19:1-2; 26:1-13). Exodus, for example, contains two collections of instruction: the ethical Decalogue, or Ten Commandments (Exod 20:1-17), and the book of the covenant (Exod 20:18–23:33). These collections include prescriptions about the altar sacrifices (Exod 20:22-26), slaves (Exod 21:1-11), personal injuries (Exod 21:12-36), social and religious laws (Exod 22:18–23:9), and Israel's liturgical calendar (Exod 23:10-19).

The commandments are given to Israel in the context of their covenant relationship with God. They describe Israel's responsibilities as members of the covenant. The covenant tradition includes blessings (which result from Israel's obedience to the commandments) and curses (which result from Israel disregarding the commandments). Some of these curses are similar to ancient Near Eastern treaties between two kingdoms, one stronger than the other.

Leviticus aims to describe holy living. It develops a holiness spectrum, moving from the very holy, to the holy, to the clean, to the unclean, to the very unclean in the realms of space, people, rituals, and time. In space, for example, this spectrum moves from the most holy place in the temple, to the holy place, to the court, to the camp, and to the realm outside the camp. Such a spectrum of holiness was designed to prepare a place for the holy God among a people who didn't always practice holy living.

Other religions had a sense of holy space, but the sacredness of holy time came first in the biblical narrative. We see the establishment of holy time in the creation story in seven days at Genesis 1, which peaks with the seventh day, the Sabbath, which is for resting in God's presence.

Day 1: Exodus 1–4

Oppression, survival, and the charge of a leader

The storyteller sets the stage for the Israelites' escape and liberation by describing the arrival of all the descendants of Jacob in Egypt (Exod 1:1-7), their growth as a people and their oppression (Exod 1:8-22; 2:23-25), and the emergence of Moses (Exod 2:1-22). Moses is charged with leading the liberation (Exod 3:1–4:17) and returns to Egypt (Exod 4:18-31).

Moses' infancy story has a parallel in the Assyrian legend (dated to the seventh century BCE) about the Akkadian King Sargon (who reigned 2270–2215 BCE). Sargon is born secretly and left in a reed basket in a river, but he is rescued by a gardener to later become king. We don't know for sure that Moses' story is informed by this parallel, but it's not unusual for biblical writers (and even among writers today) to make use of the literary forms and themes common in their world to describe their own experiences.

The Egyptians' attempt to stop the growth of the people of Israel by killing their oldest male children is in clear opposition to God's promise to the patriarchs that they would have many descendants (Gen 15:4-6). Israel's oldest males, however, are saved by the tender hands of two midwives named Shiphrah and Puah, in what could be considered the first act of civil disobedience registered in the Bible. Disobeying the mighty Pharaoh and lying to him about it was the only way to save the lives of the infants and to secure the future of Israel (Exod 1:15-22).

> **Optional:** *An additional video on God's name and Moses is available for download from* **CovenantBibleStudy.com**.

Moses' reluctance to accept God's charge to lead Israel is echoed by other prophets in the Bible (compare Jer 1). God overcomes Moses' five objections and reveals his name: Yahweh, rendered "the LORD" (Exod 3:15). This name may mean "I Am" (Exod 3:14). It may also mean "I Will Be What I Will Be," which has been interpreted by some as "My nature will become evident from my actions." The liberation program begins.

Why should a person feel reluctant to become a leader? How do you feel about your role in your family or church?

Day 2: Exodus 13:17–15:21
Crossing boundaries for freedom

Reaching Canaan from Egypt by taking the most direct route, which ran parallel to the Mediterranean Sea, would have taken about ten days. But fearing that the people would be disheartened by the expected opposition from the Philistines on the coast, God decided to lead the people through the wilderness (Exod 13:17-18). The Philistines actually settled in Canaan in the twelfth century BCE, later than the period of this story, so the mention of Philistines here reflects a detail from the author's own time rather than from the time of the story itself. The Sea of Reeds (not the "Red Sea," which comes from a mistranslation in the Greek Bible) is the final boundary before reaching freedom.

A final obstacle must be faced. As in many stories where the hero seems safe and the villain is supposed to be dead—where the villain somehow comes back to threaten the hero only to meet his final demise—Pharaoh decides to pursue Israel to bring them back to servitude.

In this story, Israel's enemies are drowned. Since we value life, even that of our enemies, what does this biblical story tell us about the value of human life?

Day 3: Exodus 20–24
Sinai covenant

The culmination of the liberation from Egypt is the establishment of a covenant between God and Israel (compare Exod 6:6-7) to make Israel a holy people (Exod 19:6). This is the ultimate purpose of the ethical Decalogue (or Ten Commandments; Exod 20:2-17), of the Covenant Code (Exod 21:1–23:19), and of the covenant ceremony itself (Exod 24:1-15a). The biblical God is a covenant God, who previously made a covenant with Noah, all of his descendants, and nature itself (Gen 9:1-17), and with Abraham and his descendants (Gen 15 and 17).

Of all these biblical covenants, the Sinai covenant on a mountain dominates the landscape of the first books of the Bible. Its instructions begin here in Exodus and continue throughout the books of Leviticus, Numbers, and Deuteronomy. It is the Old Testament's fullest description of covenant life and the covenant responsibilities that define the relationship between God and Israel. Covenant language is also an essential Christian concept in the New Testament (compare Exod 24:8; Heb 9:20; 1 Cor 11:25).

A covenant requires the fulfillment of its stipulations by the parties in order to remain valid. No community of faith that understands itself to worship the biblical God should ever forget that there are always stipulations. Not following the instructions is tantamount to breaking the covenant with God. The authors of the great history of Israel in Deuteronomy–2 Kings explain the tragic events of the fall of the northern kingdom, the destruction of the temple, and the exile in Babylon as the consequences of Israel's not complying with such stipulations.

How do you view your responsibilities within your relationship with God? What do you think are the consequences when you disregard these responsibilities?

Day 4: Leviticus 19–22
Holiness Code

Leviticus 18–26 is called the Holiness Code. In this code, the priests urge Israel to imitate God: "You must be holy, because I, the LORD your God, am holy" (Lev 19:2). This holiness applies to every aspect of Israel's life and is a consequence of faithfully observing all God's teachings (Lev 19:37). Holiness applies to the whole people in an accountable faith community.

The instructions in this chapter are very practical. They address three issues: (1) care and respect for parents, the elderly, immigrants, and the poor; (2) fairness in relationships and in business; and (3) justice in Israel's methods for settling disputes. But biblical Instruction, as an ancient collection of teachings and expectations, was written for a different place and time, and it should be read with caution. Several of these instructions, for example, apply the death penalty for behavior that no Western society would consider a crime.

How do we decide which of these instructions are still valid today and which aren't? How can the call to be holy be implemented in our society?

Day 5: Numbers 11–14
In the wilderness

Although the wilderness journey is perceived as an ideal period by other biblical writers (compare Jer 2:2), these stories regard it as a journey marked by rebellion, not only by the people but also by Moses' closest family, Miriam and Aaron (Num 12). The liberated community begins to wonder if it might have been better to stay in Egypt, and they long for the food they enjoyed there (Num 11:4-5).

We see Moses interceding before God as a prophet (compare Jer 7:16; 11:14; 14:11), but the liberated community won't pass the test of the wilderness, and their rebellions will cost them dearly. None of those who left Egypt, except for Joshua and Caleb, will set foot in the promised land. The provisions of the covenant should have been taken seriously.

The promised land isn't always available immediately after the liberation. A long and unpleasant journey usually follows. However, the land is waiting, and only faithfulness leads God's people there.

What are the wilderness tests that face communities of faith today?

Day 6: Leviticus 19:1-2
Covenant Meditation: You must be holy because God is holy.

As we read through the books of Exodus, Leviticus, and Numbers, a temptation might surface to skim over details that appear too tedious and antiquated for your attention. For most of us, lists of laws and ordinances leave much to be desired as reading material. But we should remember that these books contain some of the expectations that persist throughout the Old and New Testaments.

For this purpose, we will use the spiritual reading practice of *lectio divina*, sacred reading. *Lectio divina* has been taught and practiced by Christians for centuries. *Lectio* engages scripture through prayer and meditation, rather than study and analysis. Both approaches—study and prayer—are important, but where study informs us about the words, *lectio* forms us as a people who practice God's word. *Lectio divina* can teach us how to encounter God through the living word.

To begin our practice, locate Leviticus 19:1-2. Before reading these verses, relax and settle your breathing into a gentle rhythm. Prayerfully give to God any distractions that might interrupt your focus.

Now slowly read the assigned scripture aloud. When finished, sit quietly for a minute to let the passage rest in you. Before reading the passage for a second time, prepare to listen for a word or phrase in the text that catches your attention (resist analyzing why one word or phrase stands out for you). Read the verses a second time, and after a word or phrase stays with you, silently repeat it to yourself over and over for one or two minutes.

Next, read the scripture a third time, but with this question in mind: "How is my life touched by this word?" What feelings, images, sounds, or thoughts come to mind through the word or phrase given to you? How does your word or phrase intersect with your life right now? Use the next three minutes to consider what comes to mind.

After three minutes, read the passage one last time, asking, "Is there an invitation here for me?" Does your word or phrase invite you toward a change or response in the upcoming days? Does it nudge you toward some action or new direction? Take two or three minutes to consider and receive any invitation that God may have for you. Is there a response that you are being prompted to make?

Finally, ask God to help you hear, receive, and respond to this invitation, then close with "Amen."

Group Meeting Experience

Exodus 20:1-17 | Ten Commandments

Biblical covenants typically describe the responsibilities of both members of the covenant, God and the people of Israel, toward each other. The Ten Commandments represent the most famous list of such covenant responsibilities in the Old Testament. A closer look at them reveals the obligations Israel considered essential to covenant life.

1. How does the beginning of this covenant text (Exod 20:1-6) describe God's role in the covenant? How does this picture of God compare to the picture you have of God's relation to you in your covenant relationship with God?

2. The opening commandments (Exod 20:3-11) describe the people's obligations toward God. What are they?

3. How do the instructions to keep the Sabbath (Exod 20:8-11) connect with the creation story in Genesis 1:1–2:4*a* and with the account of the Sinai covenant in Exodus 31:12-18? How do these instructions reflect the themes of holiness and the imitation of God from your readings for Day 4: Leviticus 19–22?

4. The concluding commandments (Exod 20:12-17) describe the people's obligations toward each other. What are they? What do you think of this summary of the people's basic social responsibilities?

5. If you were to make a list of your ten most important responsibilities in your covenant relationship with God as you understand it, what would they be? How does your list compare to and differ from this biblical list?

SIGNS OF FAITHFUL LOVE

Even though we often fail in our responsibilities,
God makes a way for Covenant people
to reconcile and restore relationships.

Gospels: Matthew and Mark

GOD'S KINGDOM
Jesus reveals instructions for a new covenant community.

Bible Readings

Day 1: Mark 1–4

Day 2: Mark 12–14

Day 3: Matthew 4–7

Day 4: Matthew 11–13

Day 5: Matthew 18–22

Day 6: Covenant Meditation on Mark 10:13-16

Day 7: Group Meeting Experience with Matthew 9:18-33

Covenant Prayer

For all who cross borders seeking a better life for the ones they love

In tight circumstances, I cried out to the LORD. The LORD answered me with wide-open spaces.
(Psalm 118:5)

For all who help keep dreams alive for the orphaned, the lonely, and the abandoned

"Come, follow me," [Jesus] said, "and I'll show you how to fish for people."
(Mark 1:17)

OUR LONGING FOR RELATIONSHIP

When our new way of life is at odds with the prevailing kingdoms of this world, we look for a Teacher who has the authority over these kingdoms to reshape our lives by example.

GOSPELS

A gospel is similar to an ancient biography.

The Greek word for "gospel" (*euangelion*) is translated "good news" more than twenty times in Matthew, Mark, and Luke. This Greek word sometimes comes directly into English as *evangel*.

Matthew and Mark are examples of the same type of literature. Mark is probably the earliest of the New Testament Gospels, and so that writer is credited with inventing a new type of literature. A gospel is similar to an ancient biography, which was a very popular art form in the Roman world. Like a biography, a gospel isn't an eyewitness account, though it can be based in part on testimony from individuals who remember sayings or who interpret events they experienced.

Biographies follow the chronology of a life and use episodes to instruct and entertain the reader. The Gospels focus on the sayings and experiences of Jesus. As a framework, a Gospel includes the significant episodes of Jesus' life, death, and resurrection. A Gospel writer selects particular episodes from Jesus' life and then puts these episodes in a particular sequence. The episodes selected and the sequence of the episodes can tell us many things about the early Christian community that originally read the account.

Sometimes a teacher is tempted to harmonize the four Gospel accounts, but a better way to understand how the episodes convey important discipleship insights is to study the sayings and narratives in parallel. See, for example, *CEB Gospel Parallels*, which puts the sayings and stories in all the Gospels next to each other.

In the Bible we have four Gospels that provide distinct but comparable windows into the life of Jesus for early Christian communities. Many other gospels were written in the first two centuries after Jesus, but by the fourth century, church leaders agreed that these four Gospels were the most reliable biographical efforts to convince readers to become part of a new covenant community and thus to mature as followers of Jesus.

MARK AND MATTHEW

The author of Mark wrote the Gospel around 65–70 CE during a revolt by Jewish leaders against Rome. When he makes references to the destruction of Jerusalem in Mark 13, we think that the writer is referring to the devastation of the temple in 70 CE. Hence, the earliest of the Gospels is a work rooted in social and political conflict. The author doesn't mince words about the dynamics at play.

He immediately establishes the authority of God's kingdom at the beginning of his account (Mark 1:15), since the Roman Empire was in conflict with God's kingdom. When the author highlights this ambiguity about who is really in charge, he is expressing the discomfort felt by his church. These followers of Jesus faced the dilemma of trying to live in a world where the ways of the Roman ruling elite were in direct conflict with the way of life taught by rabbinic Judaism and early Christianity. We see this choice in Jesus' response to Jewish leaders: "Give to Caesar what belongs to Caesar and to God what belongs to God" (Mark 12:17).

Mark's church decided how best to relate to the Roman government, but they were also working out their relationship to groups that practiced rabbinic Judaism. What does it mean, for instance, to call Jesus the Messiah (or the Christ), who is David's son? This was a difficult concept for a church that consisted primarily of Gentiles. And how does God's kingdom fulfill the promises of the Old Testament?

Mark's community felt harassed. So Mark's Gospel devotes much attention to suffering and the cross, to help this covenant community learn the right way to be faithful and hopeful. These early Christians read the poems about a suffering servant in Isaiah 41–53 as songs about the faithfulness of Jesus, who suffered on behalf of his people.

Matthew's Gospel probably appeared around 85 CE. It was written for a Jewish audience, probably with some Gentile members in the community. It appears that the author of Matthew had access to Mark's Gospel and used it to shape Matthew's account. (The author of Luke's Gospel also apparently used Mark as a source.) When reading the Gospel accounts next to each other (see *CEB Gospel Parallels*), the similarities (and differences) become obvious.

Matthew uses "kingdom of heaven" language. His phrase "kingdom of heaven" means the same thing as "God's kingdom" in Mark. Matthew uses the concept so often that it dominates his Gospel account. These early Jewish Christians eagerly trusted that God is ruling here and now. They realized that God's reign has radical implications because it establishes a new covenant relationship through Jesus the Messiah, who is also resisted by the Roman rulers as the "king of the Jews" (Matt 2:2; 27:11-37).

Matthew's Gospel sets out a different order of sayings and episodes than we find in Mark's account. Matthew establishes Jesus as the fulfillment of God's promises in the Hebrew scriptures. From the genealogy to the birth narrative to his teachings of the

A Gentile is a person from an ethnic group that isn't Jewish.

Compare Mark 4 and Matthew 13.

new Torah (the covenant Instruction), Jesus is the new Moses, the new Teacher (Rabbi) from the line of David. Jesus is crowned as the ruler of the "kingdom of heaven" on earth.

Both Matthew and Mark hint at the struggles in early Christian communities who are trying to establish a sense of identity as followers of a new way of life. Matthew points to a world of predominantly Jewish believers, while Mark has an audience of primarily Gentile believers, but both communities must go about their lives in a Roman culture that serves many gods and forces all people to submit to the policies of the empire.

In the contest between two empires, Mark's Jesus comes to suffer and die on the cross as an example of faithfulness. Matthew's Jesus comes as the Teacher of the new covenant (for example, Matt 8:19; 9:11; 10:24; 12:38; 19:16). The Teacher demonstrates authority to deal with the Roman Empire because he heals the sick (for example, Matt 4:23-24; 8:2-17, 28-34; 9:18-33; Mark 20:29-34). The Teacher's power is also clearly established over the whole creation when he takes authority over destructive wind and water during a severe storm (Matt 8:23-27).

In this new kingdom that Jesus establishes, both Gospel accounts agree that the greatest ruler is not the one on the earthly throne (Mark 10:15; Matt 18:4).

When you hear the word kingdom, *what comes to mind? How does your church interact with political causes or rulers?*

Day 1: Mark 1–4
God's kingdom is near.

Mark's Gospel introduces Jesus as one who inaugurates a new kingdom on earth. This kingdom has come. It is present and near. Those who witness the appearance of Jesus, and hence the presence of God's kingdom, must respond by changing their lives and trusting what has come into existence (Mark 1:15). God's nearby kingdom requires a reaction to it. After presenting this new authority, the Gospel writer then describes how God's reign is different from the reign of the emperor. Jesus speaks of God's kingdom in parables, which are extended metaphors. Agricultural references to farming, sowing, and scattering fill Jesus' teachings about the kingdom (Mark 4:11-34). Metaphors always involve some level of ambiguity, and thereby Jesus maintains that knowledge about God's new kingdom isn't (good news) for everyone. It's a secret (Mark 4:11). This news is reserved for those who follow Jesus in this new way of life.

What does it mean to you when Jesus says, "The secret of God's kingdom has been given to you" (Mark 4:11)? Do you feel like one of the insiders? Is the new kingdom for everyone?

Optional: *An additional video on the parables of Jesus is available for download from* **CovenantBibleStudy.com***.*

Day 2: Mark 12–14
God's kingdom is not here yet.

In the closing chapters of Mark's Gospel, we encounter an alternative view of God's kingdom. The initial chapter of the Gospel announces a reign that is here right now, but the final episodes point to a distant kingdom—one that is yet to come in the future. When Jesus responds to the legal expert's question about the greatest commandment, he indicates that God's kingdom is a future ideal brought closer when we love God and others (Mark 12:34). While the answer the man gives isn't in actual alignment with then current practices for drawing near to God (sacrifices at the temple), it speaks of both the distance and the nearness of this kingdom's time and place. The kingdom is close, but not so close. Mark's account of Jesus' life makes us realize that some aspects of God's kingdom are not yet evident.

In Mark 14:25, Jesus hints at a new kingdom for a new day. While sharing the Passover meal with the disciples, Jesus specifically states that the wine will be drunk "in a new way in God's kingdom."

What does Jesus mean when he says, "You aren't far from God's kingdom" in Mark 12:34? What present-day actions cause you to think that Christians are or are not far from the kingdom? Does your church act in accord with God's kingdom?

Day 3: Matthew 4–7
New instruction for a new kingdom

Matthew highlights the difference between the kingdom of this world and the kingdom of heaven. In the temptation episode, Jesus explicitly rejects the devil's offer to bow down to him (Matt 4:8-10). In his sermon on a mountain, Jesus describes how the kingdom of heaven differs from the rule that is practiced in this world. Jesus preaches that the God of heaven has dominion over the earth. This reign has preference for the hopeless, the humble, those thirsty for doing the right thing, and for the people who make peace (Matt 5:3-9). The kingdom of heaven drives with power in reverse. In the kingdom of heaven, those who sit in positions of authority are the weakest, and those who aren't on the throne are able to exercise the greatest strength. Matthew contends that faith, not force, is the test of true leadership.

Not only does Matthew point to the political nature of the kingdom of heaven, but the Gospel account puts the role of Jesus as ruler in a new context. In submitting to the kingdom of heaven, Matthew's community doesn't need to discard traditional Jewish customs and teachings. Instead, fulfilling the Torah means establishing new covenant norms for God's people in a new setting (Matt 5:17). This spiritual and cultural renewal flows from the core teaching of God's covenant with us: to love faithfully and treat others as we want to be treated. Love your neighbor as yourself (Lev 19:18; Matt 7:12).

What does the word happy *mean in Matthew 5:3-11? (Compare the term* happy *in Psalms 1 and 84.) How is this meaning similar to or different from your feeling of "being happy" or "happiness"? Which of the teachings from Jesus' sermon on a mountain is troubling for you? Why?*

Day 4: Matthew 11–13
New way of life

Jesus begins this section with more unexpected reversals. John the Baptist is important to these early Christians (he preached about a changed heart and life), but still the greatest person in the kingdom of heaven is the least (Matt 11:11). While living under Roman rule, Jesus and his listeners knew about violence and force, and yet Jesus used that language to talk about the kingdom of heaven (Matt 11:12). This movement toward uplifting the weak and empowering those who have nothing won't come without a cost.

When using parables, Jesus offers additional explanation about the kingdom of heaven. He draws on images from the everyday experiences of his audience. The images of "planting," "seeds," "yeast," "wheat," and "landowner" describe this kingdom and help Matthew's community to see it as a reality within their grasp (Matt 13:24-43). The kingdom of heaven as "treasure" and "net" also speaks to the economic and professional status of some of the listeners in this context. Matthew's Jesus knows how to present the kingdom, the new covenant community, so that people listening will see the benefits of this new way of life. Yet Jesus is clear that not all will understand this offer. There are some who hear but "don't really hear or understand" (Matt 13:13).

Which description of the kingdom of heaven in Matthew 11–13 is most provocative, perplexing, or unsettling to you? Why?

Day 5: Matthew 18–22
Jesus is the new Teacher.

Jesus uses show-and-tell to make his point regarding the kingdom of heaven as a realm that reverses expectations. The image of a little child sitting among disciples serves to reinforce the idea of God's rule over against Roman rule (Matt 18:2). In this society, children held no political power. They were the most vulnerable, and they were considered a possession like other property. Jesus presents a new expectation for the covenant community that is rooted in childlike action and faith (Matt 19:14-15).

Humility is at the heart of this new reign, which means a practical willingness to share one's possessions. This was just as hard then as it is now (Matt 19:23). Jesus illustrates this teaching by reversing class privileges in Matthew 22. The kingdom of heaven invites the homeless people on the street to the king's banquet.

Matthew 18–22 provides more explanation of the teachings Jesus introduced in his sermon on the mountain (Matt 5). If Jesus is a new Moses, a new Teacher with a fresh set of instructions, then his lessons bear repeating until we learn the expectations of this way of life.

If you are poor, what does it feel like to be near wealthy people in our world? If you are rich, do you invite vulnerable or traumatized people to your home and your gatherings?

Day 6: Mark 10:13-16

Covenant Meditation: God's kingdom belongs to people like these.

For many of us, we are so conditioned to study and analyze scripture for what we want to know about a text that we can miss what God wants us to hear in a passage. Interpreting a reading and listening to a reading are important for our spiritual health and growth. We benefit by learning what an author wrote about life with God in the past. But it's also important to be formed by how God intends for our lives and God's life to connect here and now. Spiritual reading practices help us with this second, life-giving approach to encountering God in scripture.

So for today's meditation we listen for what God is asking us to hear in a text. It may be helpful, although still difficult, to shift from reading with our minds to reading with our hearts. For the first few times, it may feel contrived and awkward because we are not used to setting aside our analytical skills for our spiritual listening skills. So if this practice doesn't at first feel fruitful, remember that any practice takes time.

Turn to Mark 10:13-16, and read the passage silently two or three times. Read slowly, with the intention to hear all the words and to "see" all the scene. Give time to each phrase and sentence. Consider the range of emotions experienced by those in the story—the people bringing the children, the children, Jesus, the disciples, the bystanders.

Now, pray one of these prayers, or one of your own: "God, what do you want me to see?" or "God, help me to hear you through this story," or "Lord, speak; your servant is listening." Then spend a few minutes in silent reflection and prayer, staying open to whatever holds your attention from the scripture—an image, a person, a word, an emotion. Trust that this is God's word for you this day, and close with "Amen."

Group Meeting Experience

Matthew 9:18-33 | *Jesus as deliverer*

One of the government officials installed by the Roman Empire comes to Jesus because his daughter has just died. The loss of a dearly loved child is the most horrible thing any parent can experience. On the way to see the dead child, a woman with chronic bleeding stops Jesus in mid-step when he feels her touch on his clothing. This woman was considered "unclean" by all religious and social authorities for twelve years, and she trusts that Jesus can help her. Then, after delivering the child from death, Jesus heals two blind men.

1. What kind of authority does the ruler grant to Jesus? How does the ruler expect Jesus to apply his authority? What reaction would the woman expect from touching Jesus, a male, in her society?

2. By raising a child from the dead and healing a woman with chronic bleeding, what is Matthew's Gospel saying about people with the lowest status in their community? What does this episode say to the rulers of his day about Jesus' authority? What does this kind of authority mean to rulers in our society?

3. How does Jesus react when he is mocked by people who are mourning the death of the child? What did Jesus mean when he said that the child was not dead?

4. The woman touched Jesus, and Jesus touched the child and then the blind men. What meaning do you perceive in these acts of touching a person who desperately needs help?

5. The words *faith* and *believe* are used in these healing stories. How would you define these words with examples from your spiritual experience? If you believe or have faith, will Jesus heal you?

SIGNS OF FAITHFUL LOVE

Covenant people learn the surprising instructions of a new Teacher, Jesus, who delivers us from suffering, oppression, and death in God's kingdom.

Letters: Romans and Galatians

GRACE
Trusting that the faithfulness of Jesus is enough

Bible Readings

Day 1: Romans 1–3

Day 2: Galatians 1:1–3:5; 5:2-12

Day 3: Galatians 3:6–4:7; Romans 4

Day 4: Romans 5–8; Galatians 5:13-25

Day 5: Romans 9–11

Day 6: Covenant Meditation on Galatians 3:23-29

Day 7: Group Meeting Experience with Romans 14:1–15:2

Covenant Prayer

For parents who live with hardened, unforgiving hearts toward their children

Create a clean heart for me, God; put a new, faithful spirit deep inside me! (Psalm 51:10)

For parents who have learned to love their children unconditionally

Teach me your way, LORD, so that I can walk in your truth. Make my heart focused only on honoring your name. (Psalm 86:11)

OUR LONGING FOR RELATIONSHIP

Each of us is affected by the weakness of sinful desires. Our selfish desires and addictive appetites separate us from God, and thus each of us is guilty of disloyalty in our covenant relationship with God.

51

Christian greetings use words like grace, peace, mercy, *and* love.

LETTERS

Most of the New Testament consists of letters that follow the conventions for sending messages in the first century. Ancient Greco-Roman correspondence served a wide range of purposes, from personal letters dealing with situations among friends and family, to formal missives related to commerce, government, and law. Addressees ranged from specified individuals to general audiences, depending on the letter's intent, content, and tone. Normally a letter would be structured in three parts. First, in the opening, the sender and the recipient would be identified, followed by a greeting and a wish for good health. Second, the body of the letter would introduce its intent, develop the message, and solicit a response. Third, the conclusion would reiterate a wish for health or prosperity before the farewell.

While these features are found in all the letters of the New Testament, the biblical authors also exercise the freedom to depart from convention for the sake of theology and practical pastoral concerns. For example, in addition to proper names, some senders further identify themselves as apostles and slaves of Jesus Christ, and refer to the readers as those called to be God's people or as faithful brothers and sisters in Christ. The simple Greek greeting is Christianized by the use of words like *grace*, *peace*, *mercy*, and *love*. A blessing or prayer replaces a wish for good health. At the close of the letter, instead of a short farewell, it is common to find a doxology (praise of God), a benediction, or even a command for holy kissing.

According to ancient rhetorical conventions, writings fell into three categories: forensic (to accuse and defend), deliberative (to persuade and dissuade), and epideictic (to praise and blame). One or more of these elements can be found in all New Testament letters, as the writers explain the implications of the good news about Jesus Christ, affirm the readers in their faith, warn them of potential danger, and urge them to live like Christians should. Every letter is situational, written to a particular audience to address concerns in actual Christian communities of the first century. These letters substitute for the physical presence and authority of their senders, and so they become important vehicles of encouragement and training in the early church.

Of the thirteen letters attributed to Paul in the New Testament, Galatians and Romans contain the most sustained interpretation of Paul's gospel. Similar vocabulary and themes appear in both letters, such as God's righteousness, God's and Jesus' faithfulness, the works of the Law, or Instruction (Torah), Abraham's example, circumcision of the heart, and freedom made possible through the Holy Spirit. Yet Galatians isn't simply an abridged version of Romans. Each letter distinctly addresses specific issues of concern to its original recipients.

GALATIANS

Galatians shows Paul's greatest frustrations:

1. "I'm amazed that you are so quickly deserting the one who called you by the grace of Christ. . . . Certain people are confusing you and they want to change the gospel of Christ" (Gal 1:6-7).

2. "You irrational Galatians! Who put a spell on you? . . . I just want to know this from you: Did you receive the Spirit by doing the works of the Law or by believing what you heard? Are you so irrational?" (Gal 3:1-3).

3. "I wish that the ones who are upsetting you would castrate themselves!" (Gal 5:12).

With a sense of urgency, Paul asserts his apostolic authority to correct a grave misrepresentation of the gospel among the churches in Galatia. Paul is the founder of this Christian community, but in his absence some Christian missionaries have taught the Galatian Gentile converts that it isn't enough to become righteous (reconciled with God) through the faithfulness of Jesus on the cross, but that they must adhere to the teachings of the Jewish Law and circumcise all the male believers.

Paul is livid that anyone should attempt to add any requirement for salvation to the sufficiency of Christ's work on the cross. For Paul, imposing the Jewish Law on Gentile believers immediately nullifies the grace that is offered through the gospel, which is a free gift received solely and entirely through the faithfulness of Jesus, and nothing else. Salvation can't be attained by doing the works of the Law (or following the instructions of the Torah). Gentiles are saved as Gentiles, without the need for physical circumcision. Jews are saved as Jews, for whom circumcision rightly marks their election through their ancestor Abraham. There is but one gospel, one saving Jesus Christ, who addresses Jewish and Gentile believers from their different cultural and spiritual starting points.

Salvation is a free gift, received solely and entirely through the faithfulness of Jesus.

ROMANS

Paul wrote to the Christians in Rome for a number of reasons:

1. He planned to go to Spain to preach the gospel, and he wanted the churches in Rome to support the mission (Rom 15:22-24, 28).

2. He wanted to collect money for the mother church in Jerusalem, since it was out of Jerusalem that salvation had come to the Gentiles (Rom 15:25-27).

3. If the churches were to support Paul's endeavors financially and spiritually, they would need to know what Paul's gospel entailed. Romans is Paul's apology for (that is, defense of) his gospel.

4. There was tension between Jewish and Gentile Christians in Rome, and Paul addressed it as a pastor and a scholar.

The result is a long and thorough interpretation of the gospel that preserves the integrity of God's justice on the one hand, and God's covenant faithfulness on the other.

Paul begins with the universal need for salvation. There are none righteous before God, because every person is bound by the power of sin (Rom 3:22-23). Gentiles worship idols and indulge in immorality. Jews disobey God's Law even though they know what is expected of them. Without salvation, death awaits all (Rom 5:12).

A just God must deal with sin. A God faithful to the promise to Israel must save, so that other nations will also receive blessings through Israel. Both necessities are fulfilled in Jesus, Israel's anointed one (*Messiah* in Hebrew; *Christ* in Greek). Through Jesus' righteous obedience, "God displayed Jesus as the place of sacrifice where mercy is found by means of his blood" (Rom 3:25), and his resurrection has overcome forever the deadly power of sin. All who have faith that God raised Jesus from the dead, whether Jew or Gentile, can trust God as much as Abraham did (Rom 4:22-25). Following the pattern of Abraham's faith, they are made right with God and transferred from slavery under sin to freedom in the Spirit.

Therefore, God kept God's promise by sending Jesus as Israel's deliverer, the Messiah. The painful question arises as to whether Israel will be cast aside because of their rejection of Jesus. Paul is convinced that God won't go back on the divine promise because God is faithful. As long as there is a part of Israel, no matter how small, that trusts God, Israel will be redeemed and its elect status

> *An apology is a carefully reasoned, logical defense of the Christian faith.*

> *All who have faith that God raised Jesus from the dead, whether Jew or Gentile, can trust God as much as Abraham did.*

will remain intact. Paul makes this point emphatically in Romans 3:3-4: "What does it matter, then, if some weren't faithful? Their lack of faith won't cancel God's faithfulness, will it? Absolutely not! God must be true, even if every human being is a liar."

Romans and Galatians insist that salvation is a gift of grace initiated by a covenant-making and covenant-keeping God. Because grace can't be earned, no one can boast. It's only by sharing the same grace with others who trust in God's faithfulness that the unity of the church in all its diversity can be maintained.

Day 1: Romans 1–3
God's solution for the human condition

Paul begins his articulation of the gospel by putting all human beings on a level playing field when it comes to guilt before God. Paul describes sin not as a list of wrongful transgressions, but as a power that enslaves fallen humanity. Paul personifies Sin. Gentiles sin by idolatry and immorality. Jews are indicted for their pride, hypocrisy, and disobedience even with the Instruction given by God through Moses. If nothing is done about this guilt, the result is ultimate destruction for all sinners.

Out of divine grace, God has provided a universal solution for all people, Jew and Gentile, though Paul will always give priority to the Jews: "to the Jew first and also to the Greek" (Rom 1:16). Those who profess faith in Jesus Christ will be justified (made right with God), sanctified (made holy by separation from sin), and saved (from eternal destruction). This salvation is the manifestation of God's righteousness, a gift that is given apart from what is expected by the Law.

The word *righteousness* (or *right*, or *righteous*) comes from the Old Testament, and it often defines a relationship between us and God or us and others. "God's righteousness" means more than proper moral behavior. It expresses God's saving actions. "Being righteous" means that we are restored to a right relationship with God. The Old Testament God who has participated in covenant now enters into the broken world of human existence by sending Jesus to offer salvation to sinful people, so that all may be made right with God through Jesus.

In your reading of Romans and Galatians this week, when you encounter terms such as *righteousness* and *righteous* (in the CEB; or if you see the word *justification* in another translation), try reading those verses by keeping God's relationship with humankind in mind. You are saved through God's faithfulness in raising Jesus, and through Jesus' faithfulness on the cross.

How did you define righteousness *before? Does this definition change your ideas about what* righteousness *is?*

Day 2: Galatians 1:1–3:5; 5:2-12
The sufficiency of Christ's sacrifice for salvation

Yesterday's selection from Romans 1–3 provides a baseline for comparing the gospel that Paul preaches with a distorted version that is circulating among the churches in Galatia. Note that the point of contention is between some Jewish Christians and some Gentile Christians, not between Jews and Gentiles in general.

Some Jewish Christian teachers have insisted that the Gentile converts in Galatia should follow the Jewish Law so that their salvation is deemed complete. For the men, circumcision is the beginning sign of these works, but the expectation is to keep the whole Jewish Law. The misleading teachers are Christians, so they understand that salvation comes by trusting the faithfulness of Jesus Christ on the cross. Their error, however, lies in adding adherence to the Law on top of salvation through Jesus, as though Jesus' death and resurrection were somehow deficient and in need of supplement.

Paul's ire is understandable. To deny the sufficiency of Christ's work on the cross for salvation immediately reduces God's good news to a non-gospel. If following the teachings of the Law is required for all believers, then salvation is no longer a gift freely given and freely received. The Jerusalem Council had already settled this dispute and decided not to impose such demands on Gentile Christians (Gal 2:1-10). Yet the deception of Cephas and Barnabas shows how easy it is for even well-meaning disciples of Jesus to compromise God's free gift to stave off criticism and harassment (Gal 2:11-14).

What does the desire to do something to contribute to our salvation (for example, in good works or by requiring agreement with additional beliefs) say about us and the culture in which we live?

Day 3: Galatians 3:6–4:7; Romans 4
Righteousness: Abraham's trust in God's promise

Imagine the missionary opponents of Paul imposing circumcision on their Gentile counterparts by invoking the example of Abraham. They might say something like this: "Since Christians now enjoy the benefits of God's promise to Abraham, the men must be circumcised like us, the descendants of Abraham. After all, circumcision is the mark of the covenant."

Remember, Paul himself was a Jewish Christian (or, more precisely, a Christian Jew), so his debate with his fellow Christian Jews is heated. To argue that Gentile Christians don't need to be circumcised, Paul links Gentile Christians to Abraham by way of Abraham's exemplary faith. He bases his counterargument on the historical sequence found in Genesis. In Genesis 12, God calls Abraham and declares that through his descendants the nations will be blessed. In Genesis 15, God promises Abraham offspring. In Genesis 17, God seals God's covenant with Abraham by establishing the rite of circumcision. Hundreds of years later, God gives the Torah (Instruction, or Law) to Israel.

In Galatians 3, Paul emphasizes the order of these events. God's promise came first, and Abraham responded faithfully. Circumcision and the Law followed. Circumcision is not a prerequisite but a confirmation of God's promise. In Romans 4, Paul repeats this point and further highlights Abraham's trust in God in spite of his and Sarah's ages and barrenness. Abraham was deemed righteous before he was circumcised, not after. Since Jesus is the final fulfillment of God's promise to Abraham, Gentile Christians receive the status as Abraham's children because they have their spiritual forefather's faith, not because of a physical mark on their bodies.

Imagine how difficult it was for Abraham to trust in God's promise, given his circumstance as a wandering immigrant. When do you find it difficult to trust God's promise?

57

Day 4: Romans 5–8; Galatians 5:13-25
Reconciliation with God; freedom in the Spirit

What changes when a person is saved? In today's selection, Paul describes our condition before and after trusting in Christ. For example, a person who trusts God is no longer alienated from God but is reconciled to God. Every person goes from being like Adam (who disobeyed God's instruction and experienced death) to following Christ (whose faithfulness results in righteousness and eternal life). Without Christ, a person is ruled by sin, but with Christ, a person is liberated from sin to become God's servant. Only God's power that raised Jesus from the dead is strong enough to deliver sinners from the death-dealing power of sin and place them under God's benevolent rule. Life redeemed by God's grace is now empowered by the Spirit. The transfer of allegiance (from sin to God) leads to a transformed life.

What about the Law? Paul now recognizes the limited function of the Law. The Law exposes sin and shows Israel how to live. But it is a temporary custodian of our relationship with God until Christ's arrival (Gal 3:24; Rom 10:4). Even though the Law helps Israel, including Paul, to do the right thing and work toward the good of others, Paul says it doesn't have the power to save us from the effects of sin, because even the Law can be manipulated by sin to cause human beings to violate the teachings in the Torah.

What selfish desires or weaknesses have separated you from God? What does Christ's faithfulness and power over sin mean for you?

Day 5: Romans 9–11
God's faithfulness to Israel

Some claim that the Christian church replaced Israel as God's chosen people because the Jewish leaders rejected Jesus as Messiah. Paul, a Christian Jew, doesn't excuse Israel's rejection of Jesus, nor does he insist on seeking righteousness through the Law. Paul laments the misplaced zeal and ignorance of the Jewish leaders, a zeal that he once possessed. In heart-wrenching prose,

Paul expresses his deep love for Israel as he counts on the fact that "God's gifts and calling can't be taken back" (Rom 11:29).

Paul's hope for Israel is based in God's faithful love. God is merciful. Israel's special purpose is based in God's mercy and not in Israel's achievements. In the Old Testament, even when Israel was most deserving of God's wrath for breaking the covenant, God preserved the few who remained faithful. While God makes the Jewish leaders stubborn, this allows time for the good news about Jesus' faithfulness on the cross to be preached to the Gentiles. When and how will Israel be saved? Only God knows, but Paul expects that "all Israel will be saved, as it is written" in the scriptures (Rom 11:26).

Paul doesn't take sides between Jews and Gentiles. Neither one is better than the other. Both are found guilty before God, and both need salvation.

In what ways does spiritual superiority about salvation appear in our churches today?

Day 6: Galatians 3:23-29

Covenant Meditation: All are one in Christ Jesus.

This week's readings explored our relationship with God as a gift that none of us deserve. We don't deserve grace because every human being falls short of God's expectations. Grace is evident through the faithful love that God shows each of us, and God expects that we also will share this gift with others.

The message about God's grace can be shared through teaching, preaching, serving, caring, witnessing, and praying. Here we learn to pray a fragment of scripture until we realize that we are all God's children through faith in Christ Jesus. We all belong to Christ.

To begin, find a quiet place where you can spend time in meditative, uninterrupted reading. Get comfortable and focus on your breathing so that you can be fully present at this time. Turn to Galatians 3:23-29. Read these verses silently and slowly two or three times. After you have completed these readings, look back over the verses you have read, and from the words found there, form a brief, one-line prayer for your life. Some examples: "God, unlock my heart," or "I am God's child."

It's only by sharing the same grace with others who trust in God's faithfulness that the unity of the church in all its diversity can be maintained.

You could pray, "Lord, help us be one in Christ," or simply "Clothe me with Christ." Your prayer can come from any of the words or phrases in this text, because it is *your* prayer for *your* life and circumstances. Take the time you need to form this small prayer. You may need to write a few in the margin before one rises to the top for you.

Once you have a prayer in mind, sit quietly and repeat your prayer to yourself again and again for a few minutes. Trust that the prayer that comes to you is a prayer from God for you. Allow God's word to make a home in you this day through your prayer. Imagine writing this prayer on your heart. When you are ready to end praying through this scripture, simply close with "Amen."

Group Meeting Experience

Romans 14:1–15:2 | *Practicing grace*

In the five daily readings, we looked closely at God's grace toward humankind as demonstrated in the gift of salvation through Jesus Christ. But grace doesn't stop there. Only by extending the grace we have received from God to others can we truly claim to understand what God has done for us.

Extending grace in human relationships isn't avoidance of conflict or leniency without standards. When there is disagreement within the body of Christ, the integrity of grace is tested. This situation faced by the Roman congregation is a case in point. While we may no longer argue over eating food sacrificed to idols, the principle behind Paul's advice is still highly relevant if we want to grow together into a grace-filled community.

1. Many Gentile Christians in the Roman faith community, even though they were followers of Jesus Christ, had relatives and coworkers who were not. In social functions and family gatherings, these Christians came into contact with idol food, because pagan celebrations often took place in temples. At times, meat sold in the market had also been sacrificed to idols. The question arose as to whether Christians may eat food sacrificed to idols. Paul's answer seems to be, "It depends." In your reading of Romans 14:1–15:2, what underlying principle can you glean from Paul's advice? How does grace work hand in hand with sound judgment?

2. Even though the issues may not concern eating food sacrificed to idols or the observance of special days, what practices and opinions may become points of contention in churches today? What are appropriate ways to engage these disputes?

3. Paul writes, "Each person must have their own convictions" (Rom 14:5). Can this phrase be taken out of context and misused?

4. Unity is a goal and a challenge in the Christian witness to the world. What beginning steps can you take, within your own heart and your sphere of influence, to practice Christian charity and accountability without denying the diversity within the body of Christ? At its best, what does grace look like in your Christian community?

SIGNS OF FAITHFUL LOVE

Covenant people trust that the faithfulness of Jesus on the cross is all that we need to restore our broken and disloyal relationship with God.

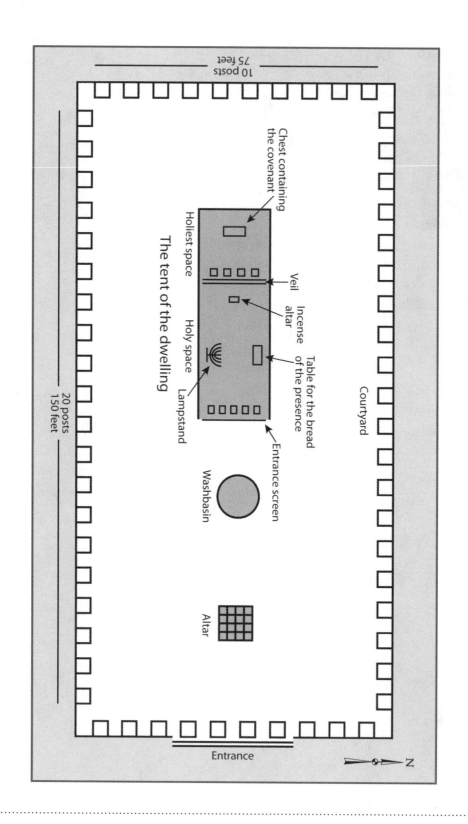

God's dwelling, a meeting tent, as described in Exodus 25 and 26

Hebrews

WITNESS
Showing gratitude and loyalty to God

Bible Readings

Day 1: Hebrews 1–2; Psalm 8

Day 2: Hebrews 3–4; Numbers 14

Day 3: Hebrews 4:14–7:28; Psalm 110

Day 4: Hebrews 8:1–10:18; Leviticus 16

Day 5: Hebrews 10:19–13:25

Day 6: Covenant Meditation on Hebrews 6:10-11

Day 7: Group Meeting Experience with Hebrews 5:11–6:12

Covenant Prayer

For those who aren't sure of God's presence or favor

He did this so that we, who have taken refuge in him, can be encouraged to grasp the hope that is lying in front of us. (Hebrews 6:18)

For those who share the gift of hospitality

Don't neglect to open up your homes to guests, because by doing this some have been hosts to angels without knowing it. (Hebrews 13:2)

OUR LONGING FOR RELATIONSHIP

When gratitude goes missing from our lives, sin separates us further from everyone we love.

HEBREWS

The principal theme of Hebrews is captured in its final exhortation: "Since we are receiving a kingdom that can't be shaken, let's continue to express our gratitude" (Heb 12:28).

Hebrews focuses on three main, interrelated topics: (1) the benefits that have come or will come to the person who puts his or her trust in Jesus; (2) the status and quality of the giver of these benefits; and (3) appropriate and inappropriate responses to such a giver's selfless generosity. The author creates a catalog of ways in which God has graced the converts in Christ:

• Providing freedom from slavery to the fear of death (Heb 2:14-15)

• The timely help of God's Son as mediator of God's favor (Heb 2:17-18; 4:14-16)

• The gifts of enlightenment and the Holy Spirit (Heb 6:4-5)

• Hope that gives them a steady anchor in life's storms (Heb 6:19-20)

• The removal of every defilement that has kept them apart from God (Heb 8:7–10:18)

• The promise of entering into the place of God's rest and full presence (Heb 4:1; 9:24), arriving where Christ has gone (Heb 2:9-10; 6:19-20), where they will enjoy their "better and lasting possessions" in their true homeland (Heb 10:34; 11:16; 12:28; 13:14)

> **Optional:** *An additional video on grace and response is available for download from* **CovenantBibleStudy.com**.

Mixed into this topic of how we benefit from grace, the author dwells on the exalted status of Jesus throughout God's cosmos. The writer stresses Jesus' matchless honor and status and Jesus' use of that status to provide reliable mediation between his followers and God (Heb 1:5-14; 3:1-6; 4:14-16; 7; 10:19-23). Both of these topics—the benefits of grace and the status of Jesus—provide the foundation for the third topic: the necessity of responding to such a giver and such gifts and promises in a way that shows appropriate gratitude, and of avoiding any response that would dishonor, and thus provoke, such an exalted figure who acted so generously.

Hebrews is anonymous. While it was attributed to Paul fairly early in its life in the church, it probably wasn't written by him but rather by one of the many other members of his team. This was someone who was much more highly skilled in public speaking and not afraid to show it (contrast Paul's philosophy of preaching in 1 Cor 2:1-5). Since it was written by a member of the Pauline mission, it was probably written to a church founded or nurtured by this mission—and therefore to a mixed congregation that had brought together both Jews and Gentiles into one church and not, strictly speaking, just "Hebrews."

This congregation, personally known to the author (Heb 13:19), had displayed exemplary faithfulness to Jesus and to each other in the face of their neighbors' hostility. These neighbors viewed the converts' new commitment to this strange Jewish splinter group as representing an insult to the many gods they once acknowledged (if they were Gentile) or a serious departure from loyal observance of the Torah (if they were Jewish). The neighbors tried a wide array of shaming techniques to bring the deviants back in line (Heb 10:32-34). Despite the shame, pain, and loss inflicted on them, the converts remained bold in their witness to the value of God's gifts through Jesus and bold in their support for each other.

With the passing of time, however, it became harder to live with the loss of status and place in society. Some converts began to withdraw from the group (Heb 10:24-25), and the author is concerned that this will further erode commitment. Such withdrawal, the author argues, is "anti-witness." It says loudly and clearly to the world that God's gifts and favor aren't worth the cost of keeping them. Hence, from beginning to end, the author magnifies the value of what the hearers have in Christ and what benefits are yet to come, so that they will want to act in a way that shows gratitude for God's costly favors and loyalty to the one, Jesus, who promises even more.

Although traditionally called a "letter," Hebrews is really a sermon that has been written down since the author couldn't preach it in person. It doesn't open with the typical letter formula seen in Romans, Galatians, 1 Peter, or 2 John (though it does transition into greetings, prayer requests, and announcements at its close). We should listen to it, therefore, as a stirring speech meant to convince and motivate. Like all effective public speaking in the classical world, this sermon aims not only to present logical argument (which it does quite well), but also to stir the hearers' emotions, to arouse confidence in the preacher's credibility, and to keep the audience's attention from beginning to end.

One of the early church writers, Origen, asked: "Who wrote this letter? Only God knows!"

The preacher wants the hearers to feel fear when it comes to choosing a course of action that would insult or bring dishonor to the God who had given so much to them.

The preacher wants them to feel confidence when they choose courses of action that show their loyalty to and alignment with Jesus, the surest mediator of God's favor. He wants them to feel a high-minded jealousy of the fame of the heroes of faith, so that they will walk in their footsteps. The emotional impact is as important as the logical content, since the preacher is looking for commitment to particular behaviors and not merely for assent to his statements.

As any strong sermon would, Hebrews calls us to deeper reflection on our lives.

How fully does your life reflect gratitude and loyalty to God? Think about a personal, spiritual, relational, or work-related issue facing you. How would a sense of gratitude (or thankfulness) affect this issue?

Day 1: Hebrews 1–2; Psalm 8
Praise for God's Son

The author's celebration of the Son's honor in Hebrews 1 serves an argumentative purpose that emerges only in Hebrews 2:1-4. The degree to which the Son is superior to the angels (established in Heb 1:5-14) is the degree to which the preacher's audience needs to pay closer attention to the word announced by the Son (Heb 2:1-4). This is the degree to which those same hearers face greater danger than that faced by people who violated the first covenant. At the same time, the Son's honor anticipates the glory that will belong to Christ's faithful followers, whom he leads to glory in fulfillment of the vision of Psalm 8 (Heb 2:5-10), and who belong to the same exalted family (Heb 2:11-13). It also underlines the exalted status of the one who has committed himself to help the converts arrive at that good end (Heb 2:14-18). The opening chapter incidentally gives a sampling of how the author finds that the "many" pieces of God's revelation in the ancient scriptures come together in the decisive revelation made in God's Son.

Who is Jesus according to the preacher, and how does he use his power and status?

Day 2: Hebrews 3–4; Numbers 14

Faithfulness and loyalty

These two chapters parallel Hebrews 1–2 in many ways. The comparison of Jesus and Moses (Heb 3:1-6), like the comparison of Jesus and the angels (Heb 1:5-14), underscores the importance of responding to Jesus' word of promise with greater faithfulness and obedience. Otherwise, one may suffer even greater loss than those who responded poorly to God under Moses (see the story of the exodus generation's failure in Num 14).

Bear in mind that the pressing issue for the preacher's audience concerns whether or not to persevere in Christian commitment (see Heb 2:1-3; 3:12-13; 4:1, 11; 6:4-8; 10:24-25, 32-36), given all it has cost them in terms of worldly standing and resources. The author places them at the threshold of entering the greater "rest" that God has prepared for God's people, namely, God's eternal realm. "Rest" is a new image for the "glory" mentioned in Hebrews 2:10 that is the believer's destiny. Jesus has already entered into this place of "rest" as their forerunner—just as his followers will if they keep running faithfully (Heb 2:9-10; 4:1; 6:19-20)!

What was the exodus generation's failure? How does the preacher use their story to interpret his own audience's situation?

Day 3: Hebrews 4:14–7:28; Psalm 110

Jesus is our covenant mediator.

One of the greatest gifts the converts have received is assured access to God through an unfailing mediator (Heb 4:14-16). The preacher offers proof of the validity of Jesus' high priesthood on the basis of a Christ-centered reading of Psalm 110 (Heb 5:5-6, 10), which leads eventually to reflection on the obscure figure of Melchizedek as Jesus' prototype (Heb 7:1-10). This foundation, together with other reflections on Jesus' sinlessness and personal acquaintance with trial and suffering, undergirds the author's promotion of the greater value of Jesus as our mediator with God. For the writer of Hebrews, Jesus is even superior to the only other available mediators in the scriptural tradition—the priests from the tribe of Levi (Heb 7:11-28).

The preacher interrupts his argument with a digression that is just as important as the main line of the sermon (Heb 5:11–6:20). He snaps the hearers to renewed attention (Heb 5:11-14), and the fact that some of their congregation have begun to slip away is proof of his hard words. In this digression, he stresses that perseverance in gratitude and in bearing fruit that pleases God is the only safe response to God's generous cultivation of the community of faith.

What reasons does the author give for confidence in Jesus when it comes to winning God's favor for us?

Day 4: Hebrews 8:1–10:18; Leviticus 16

Jesus grants us entrance to the most holy place.

The central idea in this passage hinges on understanding how limited our access to God's space was under the first covenant because of the danger that faced those who entered God's space with the contamination of sin or other pollutions (Heb 9:6-8). It hinges also on the belief that God wanted more for God's relationship with the people (Heb 9:9-10), as John captures so beautifully in Revelation (Rev 21:3-4, 22-23; 22:3-4). The ritual for the Day of Reconciliation (Lev 16) is essential background. In this ritual, the defilement of sin is removed from the people and also from the most holy place, to restore the status quo between God and Israel.

The preacher uses a ritual for the Day of Reconciliation as a model for what Jesus achieved for his followers in his death and his ascension into the heavenly realm of God. The author invokes the idea that the meeting tent was just a model of the divine realm: Jesus now plays out the ritual of reconciliation decisively on this cosmic canvas. The result is that not only the high priest, but all the people attached to this priest can enter the most holy place—no longer the cramped space in the meeting tent, but "heaven itself," God's eternal realm and full presence.

Are you confident about access to God's presence?

Day 5: Hebrews 10:19–13:25
Faith hall of fame

This section contains the famous "faith chapter" (Heb 11), which extends forward to the example of Jesus as faith's pioneer and perfecter (Heb 12:1-3) and backward to the community's own earlier example (Heb 10:32-39). Trusting God and remaining faithful requires (1) looking ahead to the unseen, future acts of God; (2) looking to the unseen but eternal homeland to which God calls us; and (3) often acting contrary to our interests in terms of this world's enjoyments. This section invites us to dig deeply back into the Old Testament and even into some of the writings between the Testaments in the Apocrypha (such as 2 Macc 6:18–7:42 for Heb 11:35*b*). Think about how each of the examples selected and crafted by the preacher reinforces these lessons.

The author continues to warn the hearers that God's investment in them, costly as it was, requires similar investment and commitment on their part (Heb 10:26-31; 12:25-29). Anything less would mean making light of God's gift and what they cost the Giver. This investment is to be shown largely in the converts' continued investment in each other (Heb 13:1-6), and in their continued willingness to bear shame for Jesus, even as Jesus bore shame for them (Heb 12:1-2; 13:12-14).

How does your congregation reflect the preacher's vision for committed community, and where does the sermon to the Hebrews challenge you to grow?

Day 6: Hebrews 6:10-11
Covenant Meditation: Grateful love serves.

Earlier in this week's episode, we learned that Hebrews was experienced as a sermon. When we read the content of Hebrews silently to ourselves, we are likely to skim, risking the loss of the poetic and oral rhythm that is often present in a sermon. The meanings of sermonic words are conveyed from speaker to listener through inflection, intonation, and emotion.

Today we will slow down and return to the spiritual practice of speaking the scripture aloud, allowing two short verses from Hebrews to become a spoken prayer. As you prepare for this practice today, find a quiet place where you can comfortably vocalize the text.

To begin, locate Hebrews 6:10-11 in your Bible. Then, very slowly, read the text out loud. Take your time; don't rush through this reading. Speak the words as though to someone who longs to hear what you have to say. Pause for a minute of silence after verbalizing the scripture, then repeat this practice. Resist going quickly, even if the pace seems awkward to you. Allow the words to form in you and from you, paying attention to emotions or memories evoked by the text. When you have completed speaking the scripture a second time, rest within a silent prayer, of gratitude.

Group Meeting Experience

Hebrews 5:11–6:12 | Honor

The following questions will help you dig into this passage:

1. In light of the defection of some converts from the congregation, what kind of intervention does the preacher expect from the more grounded members (Heb 5:11-14)? Where else does he call for such intervention in the lives of shakier believers?

2. Think about the audience's situation (Heb 10:24-25, 32-36). What is the connection between their perseverance and the honor or dishonor of God and Christ in this world (Heb 6:6)?

3. How does the agricultural analogy of Hebrews 6:7-8 reinforce the point of Hebrews 6:4-6?

4. What indication does Hebrews 6:9-12 give that the audience has been bearing good fruit in response to God's cultivation? In what direction does this motivate them?

5. Where do you find yourself and your congregation challenged by this passage?

SIGNS OF FAITHFUL LOVE

God sent us the perfect mediator, Jesus, whose victory urges us ahead and restores us on the right path among the cloud of witnesses who live faithfully.

1 and 2 Corinthians

LOGIC OF THE CROSS
Consider what Christ accomplished.

Bible Readings

Day 1: 1 Corinthians 1–4

Day 2: 1 Corinthians 7–10

Day 3: 1 Corinthians 11–14

Day 4: 1 Corinthians 15; 2 Corinthians 1:1-11; 4–6

Day 5: 1 Corinthians 16; 2 Corinthians 7–9

Day 6: Covenant Meditation on
2 Corinthians 4:7-12

Day 7: Group Meeting Experience with
1 Corinthians 13:4-8

Covenant Prayer

For the brokenhearted and grieving

Come to me, all you who are struggling hard and carrying heavy loads, and I will give you rest. (Matthew 11:28)

For the newly baptized, confirmed, and for those who have recently professed their faith in Christ

There is one God the Father. All things come from him, and we belong to him. And there is one Lord Jesus Christ. All things exist through him, and we live through him. (1 Corinthians 8:6)

OUR LONGING FOR RELATIONSHIP

At some point in life, we each will experience the lack or loss of love. We can't live without love.

71

1 AND 2 CORINTHIANS

The Corinthian culture feared shame and put a high value on honor or prestige.

Fools for Christ. That's what Paul calls the Corinthians to become (1 Cor 4:10). But they are too caught up in their posturing, their competing, their bickering, and their so-called "wisdom" to hear Paul keenly. Paul founded this church in Corinth in the early 50s CE. Corinth was no backwoods. In fact, it was the capital of the province of Achaia, and it supported a diverse population. It had much of what one would expect in an urban center: sports, conspicuous wealth (alongside much poverty), social hierarchy, diversity of religions and peoples, and all forms of entertainment, including those distractions of the seedy sort.

The Corinthian believers lived within a culture that put a high value on honor or prestige, where public boasting and puffing up oneself were key to a person's self-worth and public value. In such a culture, the loss of honor meant shame and worthlessness.

The Corinthian believers also lived in a world where there were patrons and clients. The patron was expected to take some responsibility for the client, but only if the client recognized the superiority and honor of the patron. The patronage system implies a moral obligation to help others, but the person being helped would be considered inferior.

The apostle Paul had his work cut out for him when he tried to urge the early Christians in Corinth to stop behaving like patrons toward clients. Instead, Paul insisted that these Christians become followers of a crucified Christ who offers a different kind of life. This way of life means equality for the members of the body through covenant relationships.

Paul stayed in Corinth a year and a half teaching and preaching the principles of the way of Jesus (see Acts 18:11). The Corinthian converts carried into their church many of the unhealthy social behaviors that were learned from the culture. Consequently, a few years after planting the church, Paul begins receiving letters and reports of problems (1 Cor 1:11; 16:17-18). First and Second Corinthians represent Paul's response to these issues of division and confusion that afflicted the community. He addresses questions and problems that include sexual immorality (1 Cor 5–6), lawsuits (1 Cor 6), relationships between spouses and betrothed couples (1 Cor 7), food sacrificed to idols (1 Cor 8–10), problems in worship (1 Cor 11–14), spiritual gifts (1 Cor 12), resurrection (1 Cor 15), and the collection for the believers in Jerusalem (1 Cor 16:1-4).

This church needs lessons in how to solve problems.

However, each of these situations is a symptom of the larger issue Paul must confront: This church needs a lesson in how to solve problems. Paul teaches them to stop using human reason to sort out their conflicts. Instead, he urges the Corinthian church to reason with the "mind of Christ" (1 Cor 2:16). He seeks to destroy intellectual and spiritual "fortresses," to "destroy arguments, and every defense that is raised up to oppose the knowledge of God. They [disciples] capture every thought to make it obedient to Christ" (2 Cor 10:4-5).

The pivotal solution to doubt, immoral behavior, improper worship, and conflict in 1 and 2 Corinthians is found at 1 Corinthians 1:18. Paul directs the Corinthians to the "logic of the cross." Most translations read the Greek (*logos*) as "message of the cross." However, Paul's teaching here contains more than a communication between a sender and a recipient. It's a mentality: When in doubt about anything, defer to the cross.

If anyone had room to boast, to lord his power over others, to be arrogant, surely it was Jesus. However, Jesus chose the path of humility (Phil 2:5-8) in order to build up others. "Knowledge makes people arrogant, but love builds people up" (1 Cor 8:1). Paul himself will model this Christlike humility for the immature Corinthians and then call them to "follow my example, just like I follow Christ's" (1 Cor 11:1). While he could have come among them in a lofty way, "preaching God's secrets to you like I was an expert in speech or wisdom," instead he decided "not to think about anything while I was with you except Jesus Christ, and to preach him as crucified" (1 Cor 2:1-2). In 1 Corinthians 9, Paul notes that he has all kinds of rights as an apostle (to be married; to be paid a salary): "However, we haven't made use of this right, but we put up with everything so we don't put any obstacle in the way of the gospel of Christ" (1 Cor 9:12*b*).

No doubt, like many of us converts, when the Corinthians first heard the gospel from Paul, they were bowled over to find that the gospel was all about them, that it spoke into their own lives in very compelling ways—enough to convince them to adopt this new, if strange, faith. But eventually you must grow up and learn that the gospel isn't really all about you after all. It's about being one part in a huge community across time and space. It turns out that getting over yourself can actually be a liberating experience, a gain rather than a loss. Finding yourself in a covenant community is the end goal. That goal is not based in "self-actualization." For Paul, and for Jesus before him, you find yourself only by losing yourself in the gathered community of Christ-followers.

When in doubt about anything, defer to the cross.

Paul opens the letter as expected, with a greeting that names the senders (Paul and Sosthenes) and the receivers (the church of God in Corinth). Notice that Paul here says "church," not "churches" as he does elsewhere, because the Corinthians need extreme emphasis on unity. He then offers a thanksgiving section in which he gives thanks to God for them, renews the bond across the distance, and announces the main themes of the letter. He then treats the issues mentioned above and concludes with greetings.

An earlier letter is mentioned in 1 Corinthians 5:9, but that letter is now lost to us. So our 1 Corinthians is really at least the second letter Paul sent. Clearly, 1 Corinthians didn't resolve all of the problems. Other issues appeared or became urgent, namely, the arrival of the "super-apostles" who tried to turn the Corinthians against Paul.

The second (or third) letter to the Corinthians has four broad sections. Second Corinthians 1:1-11 is the greeting. In 2 Corinthians 1:12–7:16, Paul defends his actions and his credibility as an apostle (one sent by God), and he affirms his love for the Corinthians. In 2 Corinthians 8:1–9:15, Paul gives instructions for the collection to the poor in the Jerusalem church. In 2 Corinthians 10:1–13:10, Paul offers a defense of his apostleship and closes the letter with a greeting.

In 1 and 2 Corinthians, Paul's correspondence is tied together by his desire to cultivate a covenant relationship where each person in the community depends on the other. This new mind-set (the logic of the cross) governs how the Corinthians imagine themselves as Christ's body when solving the problems we encounter in relationships.

Day 1: 1 Corinthians 1–4
Immature boasting

After offering his thanks (1 Cor 1:4-9), Paul immediately launches into a critique of the fractured nature of the Corinthian community. According to "Chloe's people," one faction has clung to Paul, another to Apollos, another to Cephas. Then there's the group that outdoes them all by claiming that they follow Christ! Paul insists that this type of competitive boasting is a sign of the Corinthians' spiritual immaturity and their tendency toward jealousy and strife. Rather than bask in the adoration of his devotees, Paul defers to the cross and makes a move toward community and humility. Models of leadership, the insignificance of their difference, and the lure of power associated with a favored leader distract the Corinthians. Paul finds their petty concerns disturbing because they limit his ability to dispense spiritual knowledge and diminish the Corinthians' opportunities to live into God's promise for their lives.

Contrary to worldly wisdom that encourages exaggerated self-promotion and selfish claims to power, spiritual wisdom is characterized by learning to depend on each other with the kind of love that can't be repaid.

Is there this kind of division in your own church? Is there this kind of division between your church and other churches in your community? Based on this passage, how do you think Paul would address the things that divide the church in your community?

Day 2: 1 Corinthians 7–10
My freedom is good, but it's not always good for others.

The Corinthian Christians believed and declared, "I have the freedom to do anything" (1 Cor 6:12). Paul agrees to this freedom, but this freedom must function according to the logic of the cross. So while "I have the freedom to do anything," it turns out that "not everything is helpful" (1 Cor 6:12). Here Paul doesn't add the personal qualifier "to me." So the issue isn't whether the action merely benefits the individual as much as whether it builds up and seeks to understand how one's individual actions might serve the community's common good (see also 1 Cor 10:23-24).

In 1 Corinthians 6, Paul advises the Corinthians to stop having sex (with prostitutes), and the next chapter (1 Cor 7) counsels other Corinthians to start having sex (with their partners). Not surprisingly, Paul indicates the normal first-century idea that a husband has authority over his wife's body; but, shockingly, he also claims that the wife has authority over her husband's body. And then another surprise: As a good Jew in a Roman society that emphasized and rewarded procreation, Paul advises against marriage if at all possible. The one concession he makes is for lust. To those who were engaged, he counseled them not to get married, because Paul believed Christ was coming back very soon (1 Cor 7:31). This also seems to have affected his advice that slaves should not bother trying to become free (1 Cor 7:21-24).

The Corinthians' questions about food sacrificed to idols is tackled in 1 Corinthians 8–10. Some Corinthians were apparently questioning whether they were "free" to attend meals at pagan temples. They argued that God is the one God, and therefore there are no such things as idols, so that food is morally neutral. However, other Corinthian believers weren't as convinced. Attending these meals at pagan temples alongside other Corinthian believers compromised the so-called "weak" believers' moral consciences. Paul uses this question to restate his position on freedom in Christ. According to Paul, your freedom as an individual follower of Jesus can't be separated from the social and moral effects of your behavior on others. All believers possess knowledge, argues Paul. But knowledge minus love results in individual conceit rather than the building up of community.

The issue in 1 Corinthians 10 is slightly different from that in 1 Corinthians 8, but the same policy prevails: When making an ethical decision, your choice depends on how it might affect the particular person or people witnessing your behavior. In one setting, it might be perfectly fine to eat the meat; in another setting, the same action might wound the conscience of a "weaker" Christian who is superstitious or ignorant. In a stunning and memorable statement, Paul says, "The weak brother or sister for whom Christ died is destroyed by your knowledge" (1 Cor 8:11). Such a person may appear to us primarily as an ignorant nuisance; to God, that same person is one for whom Christ died. As Christians, instead of insisting on our own rights, we are to be willing like Paul to "become all things to all people, so I could save some by all possible means" (1 Cor 9:22).

Sometimes we talk about our freedom in terms of "rights." Give some examples of where your right to do something infringes on the well-being of another person.

Day 3: 1 Corinthians 11–14

No person is better than another.

Two issues are addressed in 1 Corinthians 11: proper head coverings during worship and eating the fellowship meal. On the issue of head coverings, Paul lifts up three major points. First, he affirms that both men and woman may pray and prophesy so long as both reflect God's glory. Second, his argument seems to preserve, even within the sphere of Christian identity, female and male gender distinctions. At first glance he seems to follow a common cultural understanding of viewing men as having authority over women. However, in the same breath he argues for a mutual interdependence between men and women that is more horizontal than vertical (1 Cor 11:3-16).

In 1 Corinthians 11:17-34, Paul invites the Corinthians to rethink how they treat each other during the holy communion meal. Paul warns that their coming together to eat the Lord's Supper has turned into a display of divisive greed and inequity. Those who partake in the Lord's Supper with no regard for the well-being of the poor or less wealthy individuals in their community are responsible for instances of sickness and death among members of the community, and they also merit the Lord's judgment.

Spiritual gifts are addressed in 1 Corinthians 12, emphasizing their source from God and their purpose of building up community. Everyone is gifted, no gift is better or more important than another, and each gift is just that—a gift—so no one has grounds for boasting. Some gifts lend themselves to more showiness than others. Consider "speaking in tongues" (*glossolalia*), for example. That's a highly dramatic gift that draws attention. For the gift to serve the church and its witness rather than the individual, the congregation needs a translator or an interpreter. The church should always have the "visitor" in mind when it plans and conducts its worship.

How do you feel about praising someone for his or her gift?
Do you think Christians should honor celebrities?

Day 4: 1 Corinthians 15; 2 Corinthians 1:1-11; 4–6

Our faith is pointless without Christ's resurrection.

In 1 Corinthians 15, Paul responds to those who deny that there is a resurrection of the dead. He begins by reminding deniers of the tradition that he has already learned from those before him regarding Christ's resurrection and appearances. He also refers to the scriptural witness. Though the argument that Paul makes for the next fifty verses can be difficult to follow, Paul is convinced that Christ has been raised; we will be raised; death will be thoroughly defeated; we will have a sort of body that we can't yet fully discern; and God will be "all in all" (1 Cor 15:28). Nothing will exist outside of God. Ponder that.

The themes of death and resurrected life are also examined in 2 Corinthians. Notice the emphasis on affliction and consolation. Paul is afflicted, God consoles, and Paul extends that consolation to other sufferers. Who among us hasn't been rescued or at least encouraged by 2 Corinthians 4:7-9 (our "treasure in clay pots")? And as Paul has encouraged and inspired his listeners, so he expects the Corinthians to let the old things fade away and to become creatures of this new covenant (2 Cor 5:16-18).

What do you think it means to be reconciled with God so that you become a new creation?

Day 5: 1 Corinthians 16; 2 Corinthians 7–9

Cheerful generosity

In 1 Corinthians 16:1-4, Paul reminds the Corinthians about the collection of money for God's people in Jerusalem, and he provides brief instruction on taking up an offering in the Christian community. In 2 Corinthians 8–9, Paul offers more detail about the cultural and theological importance of making a contribution to support God's people in Jerusalem. First, salvation came to the Gentiles through the Jews, so the Gentiles owe something to the Jews (see Rom 15:26-28). Second, as demonstrated in Galatians 2, the collection symbolizes the unity of the church's mission, even though various branches of the church may have different people that they can see, know, or reach (Paul evangelizes Gentiles; James and John evangelize Jews). Third, those who have more than others are to give for the sake of those who have less (2 Cor 8:12-15). God loves a cheerful giver (2 Cor 9:7).

How does 2 Corinthians 8–9 affect your behavior? Reflect on the ways you give to your church and the ways that your church gives to the world.

Day 6: 2 Corinthians 4:7-12
Covenant Meditation: God will rescue us.

We return to the ancient spiritual practice of *lectio divina*, by spending time with a few verses of scripture. The intent of scripture meditation is not to teach us about a text, but to teach us from the text—to let the text transform us, rather than inform us. Both ways of accessing God's word are important for our spiritual lives—to be informed and transformed by scripture.

Our text is 2 Corinthians 4:7-12. After locating this passage, take a few moments to become quiet. Take a few deep, slow breaths, paying attention to the rhythm of inhaling and exhaling. Remember that God is as close to you as breath. Now read the whole text one time to get the feel of the passage, and then pause for a minute of silence before your second reading.

As you read these verses again, listen for a word or phrase in the passage that catches your attention. Resist any temptation to analyze or discount the phrase or word that strikes you. Contemplative reading practices are grounded in the belief that through scripture, God has a word for us, for our particular and unique circumstances, and that we can, through practice, learn to hear God's word for us. While keeping this practice in mind, spend two minutes silently repeating the word or phrase that draws you in.

Now prepare a third reading, but focus on the question, "How is my life touched by this word?" After reading the text again, take several minutes to consider how the word or phrase intersects with your life right now. What is a connection between your life and the part of this scripture that has come to your attention? Be open to any possibilities that arise.

Finally, as you read 2 Corinthians 4:7-12 one last time, do so asking, "Is God inviting me to respond in some way to this reading? Is God inviting me to some action through this word?" Ask God to help you respond. If an invitation doesn't seem clear, ask God to connect your life to the scripture in some way. Conclude this reading by placing your life in God's hands and resting there.

Group Meeting Experience

1 Corinthians 13:4-8 | *Love never fails.*

The "love chapter" is often read when a marriage covenant is affirmed during a wedding. The importance of faithful, patient, and kind love is just as crucial to a lasting commitment in the home as it is in the covenant community at church.

This faithful love requires discipline, as much work as it takes to develop deep knowledge of any subject. Our feelings about "love," a word used to describe our attachment to someone, won't last or sustain our relationships if those emotions are shallow, impulsive, convenient, or self-centered.

1. Describe a time when someone told the truth but did it in a way that seemed harsh or arrogant. Choose a couple of role models who can demonstrate for the participants how to say something hard and yet preserve love in the relationship or community.

2. What do you think is more important: to believe the right things or to do the right things?

3. Think of a time when you were jealous. What does that tell you about the relationship with the person who made you jealous? While you might recognize the feeling in a situation, how do you define *jealousy*?

4. In more than one translation, compare how Deuteronomy 5:9 is stated. What does God experience when we follow or become attached to substitutes for a relationship with God? In our

covenant with God, what evidence do we have of God's faithful love, and what evidence do we offer of our loyal love?

5. In several places in the Old Testament, a list of God's attributes is recited, which demonstrates the biblical behaviors that characterize God's covenant love. The first occurrence is at Exodus 34:6 when God passed by Moses on the mountain to offer the covenant and the Ten Commandments. Moses responds, "The Lord! The Lord! a God who is compassionate and merciful, very patient, full of great loyalty and faithfulness." Look up and discuss the contexts for several other passages that cite this covenant response: Numbers 14:18; Nehemiah 9:17; Psalms 86:15; 103:8; 145:8; Joel 2:13; Jonah 4:2; Nahum 1:3.

SIGNS OF FAITHFUL LOVE

Our hearts and lives are changed by the logic of the cross, which proves Jesus' faithful love for us.

Deuteronomy, Joshua, Judges, 1 Samuel

COVENANT RENEWAL
Refreshing our relationships

Bible Readings

Day 1: Deuteronomy 5–9

Day 2: Deuteronomy 29–32

Day 3: Joshua 1–2; 23–24

Day 4: Judges 1–2; 19–21

Day 5: 1 Samuel 13–15; 28:3-25

Day 6: Covenant Meditation on Deuteronomy 6:4-9

Day 7: Group Meeting Experience with Deuteronomy 6:1-19

Covenant Prayer

For those who feel adrift and overwhelmed

Your word is a lamp before my feet and a light for my journey. (Psalm 119:105)

For those who long to grow in love for God and neighbor

LORD, the world is full of your faithful love! Teach me your statutes! (Psalm 119:64)

OUR LONGING FOR RELATIONSHIP

We yearn for healthy relationships that generate satisfying, loyal love. Our selfish desires make it difficult to sustain relationships.

DEUTERONOMY—1 SAMUEL

Deuteronomy ends the
Pentateuch and begins
the History.

The introduction to the Torah and Genesis (Episode 1) notes that one of the four major authors who contributed to the Pentateuch was responsible for Deuteronomy. The name Deuteronomy comes from the Greek translation of Deuteronomy 17:18—a verse that requires the king to make a copy of the Instruction. The Greek translators seemed to think the Hebrew word for "copy" meant "second," and so they translated this phrase as "second instruction" or "second law."

The book of Deuteronomy is very much a second version of the Hebrew Torah (or Instruction, as it is translated in the CEB), and it includes extensive repetition of the events and Instruction in Exodus and Numbers. But this repetition is not word for word. Much new content appears in Deuteronomy. As a "copy," it is far from an exact replica. Indeed, the combination of what is old and what is new in Deuteronomy makes the book a fitting and climactic conclusion to the first five books of the Bible (the Pentateuch) because it summarizes and reiterates so much of what comes before. This summary points toward Israel's pending life in Canaan—which is taken up in Joshua and the other books that follow.

Despite its concluding and climactic function within the Pentateuch, Deuteronomy is also a hinge or pivot. On the one hand, it ends the Pentateuch, especially by recording the death of Moses (Deut 34), who has dominated the Torah since his birth (Exod 2). On the other hand, Deuteronomy opens up all that follows: the books of Joshua through 2 Kings (excepting Ruth, which in the Hebrew text of the Old Testament doesn't follow Judges). These six books—Joshua, Judges, 1 and 2 Samuel, and 1 and 2 Kings—with Deuteronomy as their introduction, are often called the "Deuteronomistic History" because they seem to inhabit the world created by Deuteronomy. They often reflect its language and themes, for example, through the repetition of key words.

An example of Deuteronomy's influence on the history books that follow is found in the way kings are evaluated in the later history of the Israelite monarchy. In the Deuteronomistic History, the kings of the northern kingdom of Israel and the southern kingdom of Judah are often deemed righteous or unrighteous, based on whether or not they centralize worship in the temple by closing down the local "shrines," which were elevated places of alternative worship. The criticism of Manasseh in 2 Kings 21 is a clear example. The imperative to center worship in one location is stipulated in Deuteronomy 12. So quite early in Deuteronomy, a test is already provided by which many later monarchs are judged and typically found wanting, leading to the nation's judgment and ultimately its exile.

These books are called history because Joshua, Judges, and 1 Samuel are concerned with the settlement of Canaan and Israel's early expansion there, first under the official leaders (or judges) and then under King Saul. But these books may also be defined by the other word used to describe this material in the present study—namely, the word *covenant*.

Covenant is a rich notion in the Bible and elsewhere in the ancient Near East. The concept is found early in Genesis in the covenants with Noah (Gen 8:20–9:17) and the ancestors (for example, Gen 15), but especially in Exodus and the covenant at Mount Sinai (which Deuteronomy calls "Horeb"). Covenant is a formal way to describe the relationship between God and God's people, in which both parties bind themselves together. It's easy to see how these covenants, but especially the one at Sinai (Horeb), undergird all that follows in the Old Testament. The covenant idea explains, for example, why the people are called to account by prophets when they go astray, as well as why the psalmists felt so free to call for God's help in prayer, especially when they felt God had neglected them. Covenant also explains:

- why Israel succeeds in the book of Joshua when they are faithful, but fails when they are not (Josh 7);

- why Joshua renews the covenant with Israel before he dies (Josh 24);

- why Israel suffers in the book of Judges when it goes astray, and how God responds to their changed hearts and lives by sending leaders as deliverers (Judg 2:11-23); and

- why obedience to God's word, especially as it is presented by the prophets, is so important in 1 and 2 Samuel, whether the king is Saul or David (1 Sam 13–16; 2 Sam 11–12).

Deuteronomy's "second" version of the covenant at Sinai/Horeb affects all else in Joshua through 2 Kings (the Deuteronomistic History). The people are judged according to the exclusive demands of

Deuteronomy 6:5 is part of the memorable passage in 6:4-9, known as the Shema ("Listen!") in Judaism.

the first commandment to worship one God alone (Deut 5:6-19; 6:4-9), and the monarchs are judged by the requirement to worship in one central place. The history presented in these books, like all history, has a point of view. This history is a passionate and even biased history, which simply means that it is *covenant history*. The presentation sounds like a sermon because it makes crucial points about what the covenant is and what it means, and what it means to be faithful to the covenant or to break the covenant. While there is more to these books than the covenant theme, everything in these books can be seen through the lens of covenant.

The notion of covenant in Deuteronomy and the Historical Books that follow includes some of the most powerful and important aspects of covenant in scripture:

1. the fundamental importance of relationship (Deut 5:2-4);

2. the sense of unmerited graciousness in the covenant relationship (Deut 7:7-8);

3. the deep commitment between the members of the covenant (Deut 6:1-9);

4. the ethical principles at the heart of the covenant community (Deut 5:6-22); and

5. the importance of loyalty or the consequences of betrayal (Deut 8:11-19).

Yet, in its ancient setting, the covenant in Deuteronomy also includes two of the most problematic ideas in all of scripture:

1. a rigid theology of retribution in which the righteous are rewarded and the wicked punished, leaving little room for God's graciousness or human failure (Deut 7:9-11); and

2. a vicious exclusion of the foreigner, so extreme at times as to mandate genocide (Deut 7:5, 16, 23-26).

The challenge for the believer now is to consider carefully how the valuable elements of covenant can be embraced at the same time that its negative applications are confronted and critiqued.

Day 1: Deuteronomy 5–9

The Ten Commandments and the greatest commandment

The Ten Commandments are the centerpiece of the covenant at Mount Horeb, also called Mount Sinai in Exodus (19:11, 23). In Deuteronomy 5, Moses retells some of the events at God's mountain and then repeats the Ten Commandments, alternative forms of which are found in Exodus 20:1-17. The importance of the Decalogue (or "ten words," another term for the Ten Commandments) is underscored in several ways. One way is that the ten words are repeated in both Exodus and Deuteronomy. Another way is that in Exodus and Deuteronomy the Decalogue appears first, in pole position, before all other Instruction. "Case laws" (Deut 6:1) that follow, for instance, are instructions that apply to specific situations, unlike the more general instructions of the Decalogue. A third way is that the ten words are also said to be the only commandments that Israel hears directly from God. That experience is overwhelming, and so, after Israel's request, all subsequent Instruction is mediated through Moses (Deut 5:22-31).

> **Optional:** *An additional video on teaching through story and interpreting the Ten Commandments is available for download from* **CovenantBibleStudy.com**.

Deuteronomy underscores the importance of the Decalogue in yet more ways. One of these is how Deuteronomy 6:1–11:32 seems to be an extended sermon based on the first and second commandments (Deut 5:6-10). Note how the great commandment of Deuteronomy 6:5 is a positive articulation of the first commandment of having no other gods. But note also how the threats to Israel's ultimate allegiance to God are discussed in Deuteronomy 6–9. They include foreign deities (Deut 7:4-5) but are mostly about other threats, including militarism, money, and morality.

Read the Ten Commandments, which are explained in Deuteronomy 5:7-21. Recall a time or two when you disobeyed these commandments.

Day 2: Deuteronomy 29–32
Old and new covenants

Deuteronomy's repetition of previous Instruction—the Ten Commandments included—isn't simple and unwavering. Moses in Deuteronomy knows that time and circumstances matter. Life in the land will be different precisely because it is life in the land, not in the wilderness. So the instructions in Deuteronomy's central collection in chapters 12–28 are often different from older teachings, repeating some earlier instructions but also revising them and updating them for life in Canaan (see Deut 12:1). Furthermore, the Instruction in Deuteronomy 12–28 seems to be developed on the basis of the Ten Commandments, another way in which Deuteronomy underscores the importance of the Decalogue. Yet even the Ten Commandments are revised! Their presentation in Deuteronomy 5 is different from that in Exodus 20, as you can see by setting them side by side and comparing them.

> **Optional:** *An additional video on the Moab covenant is available for download from* **CovenantBibleStudy.com**.

The ultimate "revision" that Deuteronomy attempts is found in Deuteronomy 29–32, which is often called the Moab covenant. This covenant is "in addition to" the one at Sinai/Horeb (Deut 29:1). Here, too, we find Deuteronomy repeating and revising—not just material from Exodus or Numbers but from its own previous chapters! Note how the Moab covenant includes future generations (Deut 29:15) in a way that the Sinai/Horeb one did not (Deut 5:3; 11:2). The Moab covenant imagines a future where humans no longer fail to obey (compare Deut 30:6 with Deut 10:16 and 6:5) because God will directly intervene to help Israel be faithful.

Over time, in the relationships that really matter to you, think about the changes or revisions needed to keep the relationship fresh, faithful, and fruitful.

Day 3: Joshua 1–2; 23–24

Moses reinvented

Today's readings form the bookends for the book of Joshua. The opening chapters pick up where Deuteronomy 34 left off, with the death of Moses. The final chapters recount Joshua's words to Israel before his own death. In both cases, Deuteronomy and its presentation of Moses has impact on the presentation of Joshua. Joshua is to be rooted in the Instruction that Moses commanded (Deuteronomy), and that will lead to success (Josh 1:7-9). Joshua is, as it were, Moses reinvented, not necessarily an upgrade (since no one compares to Moses; see Deut 34:10-12), but a new version. The balance of Joshua 1–2 shows how Joshua's fidelity (loyal love) rubs off on Israel (Josh 1:10-18) and how Israel's fidelity, in turn, affects the inhabitants of the land, even leading to Canaanite "professions of faith" (Josh 2:8-13; 6:25).

Joshua 23 and 24 comprise Joshua's last will and testament, and are quite similar (though much shorter) than Moses' final words in the book of Deuteronomy. Like Moses, Joshua is at pains to ensure that the people remain faithful to God after his death. Israel's obedience is a response to all that God has done (Josh 23:3, 9, 14), but is nevertheless mandated and essential (Josh 23:6, 11), lest things end in disaster (Josh 23:15-16). This is why Joshua puts the covenant question to Israel in Joshua 24 with his famous statement, "Choose today whom you will serve," and also why he follows Moses' example once more by setting an example himself: "But my family and I will serve the Lord" (Josh 24:15).

Whom do you serve? How do you know?

Day 4: Judges 1–2; 19–21

Downward spiral

Judges tells the story of Israel after Joshua, and it isn't always pretty. The first chapter comes as a surprise after reading Joshua. Not everything went smoothly in the settlement of the land. Instead, much work remains to be done (Judg 1:1). Moreover, the official leaders (also called judges) are chieftains who arise to deliver Israel from its oppressors after it has gone astray from God.

These deliverers are charismatic military and religious leaders who rarely "judge" in the formal, legal sense (for example, Judg 2:16-19), and they never attain to Joshua's status, let alone Moses'. If anything, the leaders whose lives are described in this book seem to get worse as time passes. After the successful leaders Othniel, Ehud, and Deborah, we read stories about the ambiguous careers of Gideon and Jephthah, as well as the seemingly self-centered exploits of Samson, who "delivers" Israel only at the end of his life and then only, it would seem, as an act of revenge (Judg 16:28).

The ultimate decline is found in the final chapters of Judges, which recount the horrific story of the rape and dismemberment of a Levite's secondary wife, which leads to intertribal warfare and the near annihilation of the tribe of Benjamin for its role in the atrocities. The Benjaminites are saved by actions that are every bit as disturbing as the Israelites' conquest of Canaan, though this time the Israelites turn inward against Israel's own territory and people (Judg 21:1-12, 16-24). Observe the marked absence of God's direct activity in these chapters—the exception being God's approval of punishing action against the Benjaminites for their crime (Judg 20:18, 23, 28, 35; 21:15). It is as if God stands back at the end of Judges, leaving Israel to its own devices (and vices). We see, in the process, the terrifying results of life lived outside of covenant.

Think of a harmful leader at work or at school or in government. Which of this leader's deeds have seemed to violate expectations and relationships? Now think of a leader who inspires. What behaviors have exceeded expectations?

Day 5: 1 Samuel 13–15; 28:3-25
Tragedy of King Saul

The end of Judges portrays Israel in dire straits, with each person doing "what they thought to be right" (Judg 17:6; 21:25). That's a far cry indeed from Deuteronomy's emphasis on careful obedience to God's covenant, rather than to one's own whims. This phrasing in Judges, then, is proof of Israel's covenant disobedience.

But the end of Judges also indicates that this situation was due to the fact that "in those days there was no king in Israel" (Judg 17:6; 18:1; 19:1; 21:25). Israel is not only disobedient but unruly (un-ruled), guided neither by God nor by a representative of God such as a king or a prophet. First Samuel recounts the rise of both kinds of representative leaders.

> **Optional:** *An additional video retelling the story of Hannah and the infant Samuel is available for download from* **CovenantBibleStudy.com**.

The opening chapters tell of the birth and early career of Samuel, who is the last of the chieftain leaders and the first of the prophets. He is also God's kingmaker, anointing Saul the first king of Israel. From its inception, kingship is portrayed as a highly ambivalent institution, one that is ultimately in tension with God's rule (1 Sam 8:7). Not surprisingly, then, the first king, Saul, is a tragic figure from the start. It does come as a surprise, if not an act of mercy or grace, that he comes from the tribe of Benjamin (1 Sam 9:1, compare the end of Judges).

Saul sacrifices when he shouldn't have (1 Sam 13), makes a rash solemn pledge that could have led to the death of his own son (1 Sam 14), and then breaks the rules of holy war and lies about it after the fact to Samuel (1 Sam 15). All this leads to Saul's rejection as king (1 Sam 13:13-14; 15:23), because God is seeking a man "of his own choosing" (or, "after his own heart"; 1 Sam 13:14). That turns out to be David, of course (1 Sam 16), but note that the prediction of Saul's demise is made long before David is anointed and even longer before David's own significant disobediences to God's commands (2 Sam 12). In the end, Saul breaks the very religious rules he himself instated by consulting a spiritual medium in order to get dead Samuel's advice one last time (1 Sam 28:3-28). Saul dies a dishonorable death thereafter (1 Sam 31).

When human beings form a community, why do we seek a chief, or king, or president? How does this affect our covenant relationship with God?

Day 6: Deuteronomy 6:4-9

Covenant Meditation: Renewing the covenant

Again we have an opportunity to experience scripture by allowing the word to form us through and in our hearts. To mature spiritually, our heads and hearts must be engaged by the living word.

This spiritual way of reading scripture has been practiced in Christian communities for centuries. The classic name for this ancient way of reading the Bible is *lectio divina*, which in Latin means "divine reading." Traditionally in divine reading, there are four key movements through which we listen to a brief selection of scripture: reading, meditating, praying, and resting (contemplating) in God's word.

The meditation is Deuteronomy 6:4-9, in which Moses reaffirms that the holy covenant between God and God's people for all generations is forged and sustained in the commandment to love God always and completely. Open your Bible to this scripture, and mark its location. Go to as quiet a place as possible for this reading, and get comfortable where you are seated. Place both feet on the ground and breathe slowly in and out until you have a sense of calmness and have, as best you can, set aside distractions that are on your mind about other matters.

Read the passage slowly, aloud or silently, paying attention to the whole text—every sentence, phrase, and word. Approach the scripture as though it is new to you. When finished, wait in a minute of silence.

Read the passage again, now listening for one word or phrase that catches your attention. Try not to analyze why a specific word or phrase stands out to you, but receive it as something God invites you to hear. If desired, write this word or phrase in your workbook. Take three minutes of silence to reflect on what caught your attention. What does this word or phrase bring to mind for you? Let your mind engage with the word or phrase and consider what it means to you right now. Resist editing your thoughts, and do not rush through this silent time. It may feel like an hour to you at first, but stay with the full three minutes if you can. For some, this silent time is easy, but for others it can seem to take forever. Try to grow in this practice of silence before God with the scripture.

Read the scripture one last time. Now reflect on feelings or memories your word or phrase evokes. Does your word or phrase point to something that you or someone you know longs for or needs? In as much or as little silent time as you need, write down any reflections that come to your mind or heart.

When you are ready, in prayer offer back to God all that you have heard, thought, and felt in this spiritual reading practice. Entrust to God any insights, questions, worries, or longings that this scripture brings to light for you. Before you end this time of praying the scripture, ask yourself if you sense an invitation from God to act or respond in some way. There may be a small invitation (for example, to attend worship) or a broad one (to pray each day), or you may not yet sense an invitation. You may discover later in the day or week that something comes back to you from this experience. A word or phrase may drift up from your heart or memory for you to reflect upon at another time. There is no right or wrong way to do this practice. It is simply one way to spend time with God and God's message in quiet, personal reflection.

Group Meeting Experience

Deuteronomy 6:1-19 | *A portrait of the covenant*

The book of Deuteronomy provides us with yet another way of describing the covenant between God and God's people and defining the nature of community within such a covenant. Because this covenant provides the theological lens for the historian's evaluation of Israel's faithfulness in the books that follow—Joshua, Judges, 1 and 2 Samuel, and 1 and 2 Kings—it plays a major role in the way we understand much of biblical history and thought.

1. Biblical covenants describe community relationships in which members share mutual care for and obligations to each other. What are the human responsibilities and obligations in this covenant? What are the divine responsibilities and obligations?

2. In what ways is Deuteronomy's covenant similar to and different from the biblical covenants you have already studied in Genesis and Exodus?

3. "Love" in Deuteronomy 6:5 is a term taken from kinship and family relationships in the ancient world. What role does it play in the

relationship between God and Israel in the Deuteronomic covenant? What attitudes and actions does it include?

4. How do you think the author of Luke intends us to understand this kind of covenant love when he quotes Deuteronomy 6:5 in his introduction to the parable of the good Samaritan (Luke 10:25-37)? Compare Matthew 22:34-40.

5. This covenant is built on a theology of rewards and punishments (Deut 6:3, 14-19). What do you see as the strengths and weaknesses of such a theology?

6. What aspects of Deuteronomy's covenant and of its ancient world do you find problematic for our understanding of covenant today? What aspects do you find life-giving and insightful for faithful community life?

SIGNS OF FAITHFUL LOVE

We don't deserve God's love because we are unfaithful,
but Covenant people are restored and reinvented
through God's unexpected favor.

Well done!

You have completed the first participant guide, *Creating the Covenant*. You studied daily from scripture about the importance of establishing a covenant with God and others. In your Covenant group, you planted the signs of faithful love that are present among friends. Relationships are growing.

About now you are probably wondering whether to continue the daily readings from scripture. Even if you are feeling stress from a hectic life, you can probably see the spiritual benefit of sharing expectations, divine promises, and personal yearnings with your Covenant group.

Keep going! You can do it. The Bible is a big, ancient collection of books, and getting the "big picture" for the whole Bible will help you grow (produce fruit) and become more faithful as a friend, parent, co-worker, or leader. The loyal relationships that can be cultivated in a Covenant group will produce fruit for the rest of your life.

Whether your group takes a break or continues right away, *Living the Covenant* is waiting for your input. You now understand how the biblical God relates to us through covenant. In the second participant guide, you will learn effective strategies for covenant living with others.